CAREER

Pathways®
Employment Essentials

APPLICATIONS | RESUMES | COVER LETTERS

ISBN 978-1-934350-44-7

PAXEN
Learning Corporation

Melbourne, Florida
www.paxen.com

Acknowledgements

▶ **Photo Credits**

Cover (job interview) © Ariel Skelley/Blend Images/Corbis **iii (businessman using laptop)** iStockphoto © Kristian Sekulic **iii (hand and pen with resume)** iStockphoto © Pixsooz **iii (woman typing cover letter)** iStockphoto © 4FR **iv (woman in library)** iStockphoto ©René Mansi **iv (women at computer)** iStockphoto © THEGIFT777 **x (store clerk)** iStockphoto © Sean Locke **x (carpenter)** iStockphoto © Robert Cocquyt **xi (computer technician)** iStockphoto © Darren Wise **xi (EMT and patient)** iStockphoto © Kerrie Kerr **xi (educator)** iStockphoto © René Mansi **1 (woman completing application)** iStockphoto © Jamie Wilson **1 (man at computer)** iStockphoto © Mark Bowden **2 (job fair)** Getty images © George Doyle **2 (man completing application)** iStockphoto © DWlabsInc **2 (woman at kiosk)** © Paxen Learning. Special thanks to Jenifer Harrison and Sandra Bruner **2 (businessman using laptop)** iStockphoto © Kristian Sekulic **2 (woman completing application)** iStockphoto © Jamie Wilson **2 (man at computer)** iStockphoto © Mark Bowden **3 (man at computer)** iStockphoto © David Hills **3 (silhouette)** iStockphoto © A-Digit **3 (magnifying glass with document)** iStockphoto © Lumpynoodles **3 (silhouette man using laptop)** iStockphoto © Illustrious **19 (man dressed business-casual)** Shutterstock © Yuri Arcurs **19 (woman dressed business-casual)** iStockphoto © 4x6 **21 (couple remodeling a home)** iStockphoto © Phillip Spears **21 (appliances)** iStockphoto © JazzIRT **21 (family gardening)** iStockphoto © kristian sekulic **21 (tools)** iStockphoto © mattjeacock **23 (doors and windows)** iStockphoto © M. Eric Honeycutt **23 (woman cleaning window for installation)** iStockphoto © George Peters **23 (woman at kiosk)** © Paxen Learning. Special thanks to Jenifer Harrison and Sandra Bruner **24 (man reviewing online application)** iStockphoto © Michael Phillips **25 (silhouettes)** iStockphoto **26 (pen)** iStockphoto © Murat Giray Kaya **26 (employment application and pen)** iStockphoto © surfertide **26 (man completing application)** iStockphoto© wdstock **27 (job application form, filling with a pen)** iStockphoto © enis izgi **27 (man looking over papers)** iStockphoto © Ivan Solis **33 (woman working in home office)** iStockphoto © Mark Bowden **33 (hand and pen with resume)** iStockphoto © Pixsooz **33 (managers reviewing resume)** iStockphoto © SelectStock **34 (woman working in home office)** iStockphoto © Mark Bowden **40 (solar panel installer)** iStockphoto © Elena Elisseeva **41 (silhouettes)** iStockphoto **42 (silhouettes)** iStockphoto **43 (computer technician)** iStockphoto © Darren Wise **44 (silhouettes)** iStockphoto **45 (educator)** iStockphoto © René Mansi **46 (store clerk)** iStockphoto © Sean Locke **48 (carpenter)** iStockphoto © Robert Cocquyt **50 (EMT and patient)** iStockphoto © Kerrie Kerr **56 (hand and pen with resume)** iStockphoto © Pixsooz **66 (managers reviewing resume)** iStockphoto © SelectStock **70 (architect at computer)** iStockphoto © Kryczka **70 (architect reading blueprint)** iStockphoto © Diego Cervo **71 (Tuscan stone home)** iStockphoto © Lisa-Blue **71 (contemporary pool home)** iStockphoto © ShutterWorx **71 (stone home with balcony)** iStockphoto © Spencer Doane **71 (home with arched entry and palm trees)** iStockphoto © Marje Cannon **71 (tri-level home)** iStockphoto © Christophe Testi **71 (home with patio)** iStockphoto © Chuck Schmidt **71 (home with steps to balcony)** iStockphoto © Ursula Alter **71 (home with driveway)** iStockphoto © Pamspix **71 (Spanish-style home with chimney)** iStockphoto © Ziggymaj **77 (man at laptop computer)** iStockphoto © Mark Bowden **77 (woman typing cover letter)** iStockphoto © 4FR **77 (hands on keyboard)** iStockphoto © Huchen Lu **77 (envelope and pen)** iStockphoto © Alex Kotlov **78 (man at laptop computer)** iStockphoto © Mark Bowden **84 (woman typing cover letter)** iStockphoto © 4FR **98 (silhouettes)** iStockphoto **99 (silhouettes)** iStockphoto **120 (envelope and pen)** iStockphoto © Alex Kotlov **120 (laptop computer)** iStockphoto © Alex Slobodkin **121 (hands on keyboard)** iStockphoto © Huchen Lu **121 (hiring official)** © Paxen Learning. Special thanks to Veronica Massa and Jenifer Harrison

Table of Contents

2
Today, nearly everyone who applies for a job must complete an application.

56
Candidates may use a variety of resume formats to optimize their candidacy.

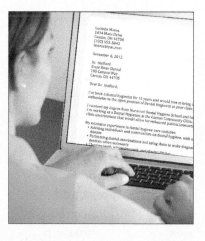

84
A well-written cover letter should encourage a hiring official to read your resume.

About Career Pathways

What do you want to be when you grow up? It's an innocent question, one often asked of schoolchildren. Increasingly, though, as our economy changes—and with it, entire industries—people of all ages are asking the same question. From children to young adults and on to older professionals and dislocated workers, more people than ever are attempting to find their way in today's workplace.

Often, the journey begins after high school. Whether they earn a diploma or a GED credential, potential employees often lack the proper support and guidance to make the transition from school to the workplace.

Adding to the challenge, workplaces themselves are changing. Traditional industries that once employed generations of workers have struggled to survive. Amid intense competition for available jobs, job seekers who lack necessary certifications or degrees and/or soft and career-specific skills struggle to find lasting success.

In short, today's workers face a number of specific challenges. For example:

- Many workers, though highly skilled, may lack a market for their services.

- Although workers may have years of on-the-job experience, they could be unaware of current job-seeking techniques, such as using the Internet and in-person networking.

- Similarly, job seekers may lack a current, polished resume or sharp interviewing skills.

The solution to these challenges can be quite complex. To help people determine their next steps, Paxen offers its newest series, *Career Pathways*. This product line provides learners with strategies to survive—and thrive—in a 21st-century workforce.

Titles such as *Transitions, Job Search, Employment Essentials,* and *Green Jobs* aid learners in exploring and narrowing options. Others, such as *Effective Employee, Document Literacy,* and *Financial Literacy,* provide strategies for excelling inside and outside of the workplace.

Career Pathways was built in accordance with the work-readiness competencies listed in the table below.

COMPETENCIES

Pathways Essential Knowledge and Skill Statements	National Standards in K-12 Personal Finance Education
Comprehensive Adult Student Assessment Systems (CASAS)	Workforce Investment Act (WIA) Elements
Equipped for the Future (EFF)	21st Century Skills
National Career Development Guidelines (NCDG)	Pre-Employment and Work Maturity (PEWM)

CAREER Pathways®

The Next Generation of Work-Readiness Materials

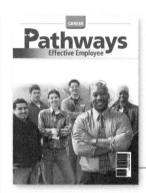

▶ *Effective Employee*

Effective Employee equips emerging professionals with the skills, experiences, and intangibles to excel and advance in today's workplace. An engaging narrative and high-interest features help learners unlock the secrets to lasting success.

▶ *Job Search*

Job Search removes the mystery—and guesswork—from the employment process. Learners receive instruction in key areas—from authoring resumes and cover letters to refining interviewing and negotiating skills—critical to employment success.

▶ *Document Literacy*

In *Document Literacy*, we put fine print under the microscope. A series of detailed callouts help learners decode and master complex consumer, personal, business, and financial documents. Chapter reviews allow learners to check understanding.

▶ *Green Jobs*

Stuck in a rut? Want a better future? Then *Green Jobs* is the resource for you. Packed with information, activities, and a closing career plan, *Green Jobs* provides insight into one of the fastest-growing areas of the United States economy: green industries.

About Employment Essentials

For the Learner

Today's industries—and employer needs—are shifting at light speed. *Employment Essentials* helps job seekers keep pace and even get ahead through a series of contemporary strategies designed to produce eye-catching applications, resumes, and cover letters. *Employment Essentials* uses an engaging narrative and various components to enhance the learning experience.

1 Each lesson begins with a list of student achievement goals and key terms.

3 High-impact images and graphics visually reinforce the narrative.

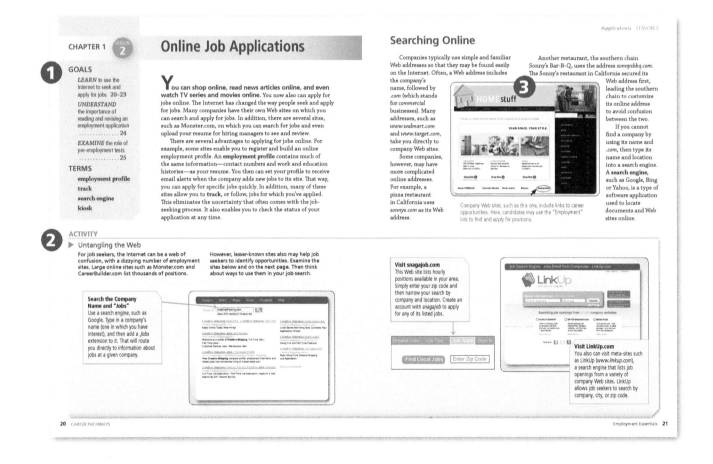

2 Activities offer students insights into leading employment strategies.

Pathways Features

Each chapter highlights one essential work-related topic in a special Pathways feature. These features offer in-depth information about how topics introduced in the chapter impact specific career areas.

> **1** Pathways features enable students to explore concepts with their own career goals in mind.

> **2** Learners receive in-depth understanding of best practices in the job search process.

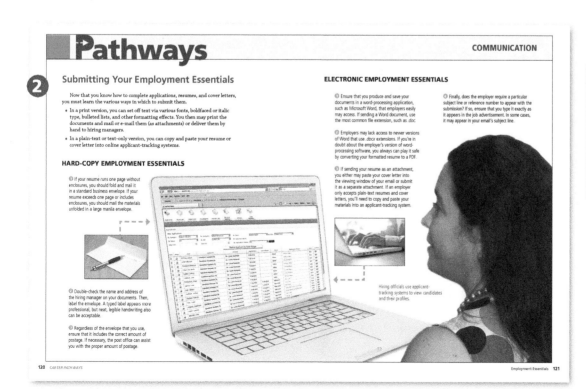

Lesson and Chapter Reviews

Each lesson closes with a review that assesses learner progress. Each chapter concludes with a checklist that gauges mastery and a review that enables students to assess their knowledge of employment concepts. These pages may be removed and submitted for assessment purposes.

1 Lesson review questions correlate to learning goals at the start of each lesson. Students should write their answers on a separate sheet of paper.

2 Items in each recap mirror goals listed at the start of each lesson.

3 The first page of the chapter review contains several types of questions: matching, true or false, multiple choice, and short answer.

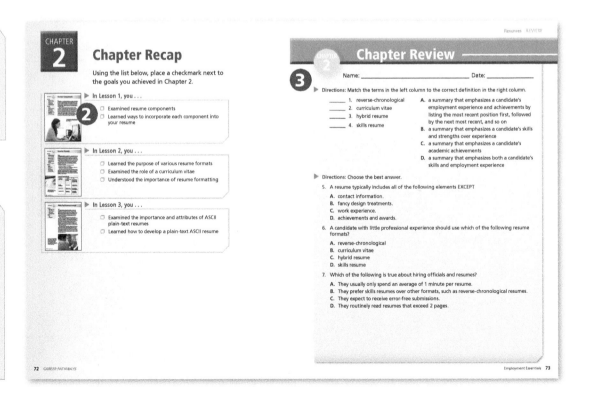

Chapter Review Activities

Chapter review activities enable students to participate in and receive practice with real-life employment scenarios. Such scenarios include completing a job application, authoring a resume, and writing a cover letter.

1 These activities allow learners to practice the successful completion of employment documents.

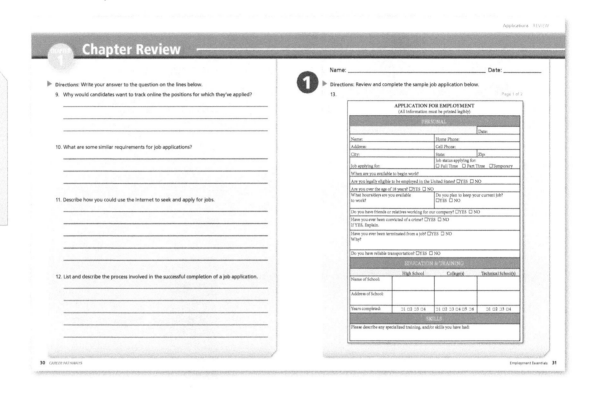

2 Learners complete the various components that together comprise a resume and a cover letter.

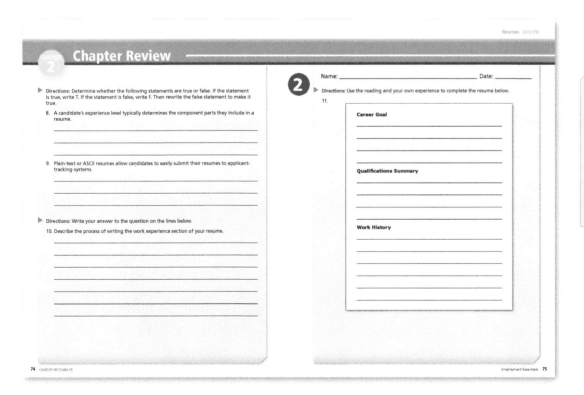

Character Introduction

Throughout *Employment Essentials,* we aim for authenticity. For that reason, we've developed a series of characters—all from different backgrounds and with different career goals—that you'll follow throughout this book. Below and on the next page, you'll meet five fictitious characters: Clive, a customer service representative; Anu, a carpenter's apprentice; Sandra, an information technology support associate; Luis, an emergency medical technician (EMT); and Jacinda, a program coordinator for English as a Second Language (ESL) and English language learners (ELL). As you progress throughout *Employment Essentials*, you'll note their progress—as well as your own.

CLIVE ROBINSON

CURRENT POSITION: Customer Service Representative
OBJECTIVE: Hotel Clerk
LONG-TERM GOAL: Degree in Business Management

EDUCATION	High School
	Some college coursework toward degree in Business Management
EXPERIENCE	One year working in customer service at a retail store; no hotel experience

ANU KHOSIA

CURRENT POSITION: Carpenter's Apprentice
OBJECTIVE: Commercial Carpenter
LONG-TERM GOAL: Master Carpenter

EDUCATION	GED credential
	Earned carpenter's certification
EXPERIENCE	Four years as a carpenter's apprentice

CURRENT POSITION: Support Associate
OBJECTIVE: Technical Support Team Member
LONG-TERM GOAL: IT Network Specialist

EDUCATION	High school diploma
	Associate's (AAS) degree in Computer Servicing Technology
EXPERIENCE	Three years working in community college computer department while earning AAS degree

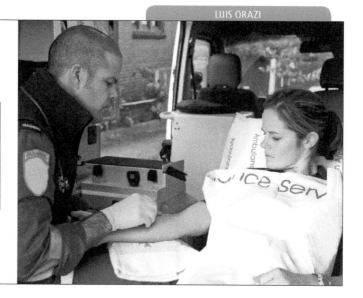

CURRENT POSITION: EMT
OBJECTIVE: EMT Supervisor
LONG-TERM GOAL: EMT Supervisor

EDUCATION	Basic EMT certification
	Advanced EMT certification
EXPERIENCE	Volunteer firefighter
	Two years as an EMT

CURRENT POSITION: ESL/ELL Program Coordinator
OBJECTIVE: Assistant College Professor
LONG-TERM GOAL: National expert on ESL/ELL teaching strategies

EDUCATION	ESL paraprofessional certification	Master's (MA) in Educational Leadership
	Bachelor's (BS) degree in Education	Doctorate (Ed.D.) in Educational Leadership
EXPERIENCE	ESL paraprofessional	District ESL itinerant teacher
	Classroom teacher	ESL/ELL program coordinator
	Resource teacher	

Applications

Chapter Recap	Chapter Review
☑ _____	_____
☑ _____	_____
☑ _____	_____

Job Application Preparation

GOALS

TERMS

job application

components

applicant-tracking system

For many, a job search is more of a marathon than a sprint. Just like marathoners, job seekers train for the larger competition by first completing smaller exercises. A key, early step in the race for employment involves the completion of all forms and paperwork, including job applications. A **job application** is a print or electronic form that potential employees must complete to be considered by a company for employment.

Job applications usually include many of the same **components**, or parts. However, because each company develops and uses its own job application form, some components may differ from one application to another. Another difference involves the amount of candidates who complete applications. In the past, a candidate might have completed a job application only if he or she were applying for a part-time or an hourly position. Today, however, nearly everyone who applies for a position—whether white-collar or blue-collar or full- or part-time—must complete an application. Often, companies require applications so that they can comply with state or federal hiring laws.

Most employers today require candidates to complete a job application.

Following Directions

A large part of applying for jobs involves following directions. For example, employers may require the completion of certain informational fields on applications. Sometimes, these fields are noted by stars or asterisks (*). You must complete all mandatory fields before an applicant-tracking system (ATS) will accept your electronic application. An **applicant-tracking system** is an electronic employer database that collects, stores, and sometimes even ranks applicant information. Most large companies today use applicant-tracking systems to receive application materials.

As an applicant, you should seek to comply with employer submission requirements. For example, employers may prefer that candidates submit materials to their ATS rather than emailing them directly to hiring officials. Employers tend to view an employment application as they would a work assignment. If you're unable to follow directions at this point, they may wonder how well—or whether—you could follow directions on a work assignment.

Job applications come in all shapes and sizes. On the pages that follow, you will see five different types of job applications. Each application contains both similarities and differences. As the table below indicates, most applications require basic information. Many also often ask for career-specific information that helps employers understand your range of qualifications. Some of them also may include an industry- or job-specific test designed to measure applicant abilities.

TYPES OF APPLICATION FORMS

Type	Description
Basic	Most employment applications consist of only one or two pages of standard questions. Basic forms ask for your personal and contact information, such as your full legal name, date of birth, driver's license numbers, Social Security number, street and email addresses, and phone numbers. Remaining fields ask for employment information from your two most recent jobs, education history, and availability to work. Nearly every application will ask whether you're legally authorized to work in the United States and whether you've ever been convicted of a crime.
Detailed	Many employers today use more detailed application forms in the hiring process. These detailed forms include all of the basic elements while also gathering more job-specific information, such as your knowledge of a certain software or specific certifications you may hold. Almost all of these forms contain a separate section in which you may authorize (by your signature) a business to run a criminal background and even a credit check.
Tests	Some hard-copy or paper applications may include basic test questions in relevant subjects such as math. However, most application testing occurs online. After you provide your information and work and education histories, the automated application will direct you to a final testing portion. These tests feature multiple-choice questions designed to evaluate your aptitude, personality, and interests. The company then can compare the results on your test with the results of other applicants.

Sample Application 1

Clive Robinson earned his high school diploma and has worked in retail customer service ever since. However, Clive recently decided to change careers to hotel management. He plans to study for a bachelor's degree in hospitality management and also to apply for a front-desk position at a hotel, which will give him valuable experience in his new career field.

❶ *S.S. # refers to a person's Social Security number. Companies use Social Security numbers to conduct background checks on candidates applying for positions.*

❷ *The greater your availability, the higher the likelihood that you'll land a position. For many jobs, such as those in hospitality management, you may be required to work on weekends. By offering flexibility in your schedule, you show a willingness to put the company's needs ahead of your own.*

❸ *Some applications ask you to list friends or relatives who work at the company. To avoid any conflict of interest, the company will want to ensure that, if hired, you will not supervise, or be supervised by, a friend or relative.*

CLIVE • SERVICE

The Queen's Inn — APPLICATION FOR EMPLOYMENT

PERSONAL

Date: 9/17/12

Name: Clive T. Robinson ❶ S.S. # XXX-XX-XXXX

Address: 7254 Ashland Ave. — Phone: (555) 543-7504

City: Raeford — State: NC — Zip: 28376

Job applying for: Front desk clerk

Job status applying for: ☑ Full Time ☐ Part Time ☐ Temporary

When are you available to begin work? Immediately

Are you legally eligible to be employed in the United States? ☑ YES ☐ NO

Are you over the age of 18 years? ☑ YES ☐ NO

❷ What hours/days are you available to work? Sunday through Saturday, day and evening hours

Do you plan to keep your current job? ☐ YES ☑ NO

❸ Do you have friends or relatives working for our company? ☐ YES ☑ NO

Have you ever been terminated from a job? ☐ YES ☑ NO Why?

Do you have reliable transportation? ☑ YES ☐ NO

EDUCATION & TRAINING

	High School	College(s)	Technical School(s)
Name of School:	Raeford High School		Sandhills Community College
Address of School:	178 Mt. Curve, Raeford, NC		3395 Airport Rd., Pinehurst, NC
Years completed:	☐1 ☐2 ☐3 ☑4	☐1 ☐2 ☐3 ☐4 ☐5 ☐6	☐1 ☐2 ☐3 ☐4

SKILLS

❹ Please describe any specialized training, and/or skills that would assist us in evaluating your application:
I have had extensive training in using POS cash register systems, hardware, and software. I feel confident in my ability to apply that knowledge to other systems.

Page 1 of 2

❹ *Use opportunities such as this one to spotlight any specific certifications or skills that you possess. In so doing, emphasize their relevance to the position for which you're applying.*

Sample Application 1, *page 2*

CLIVE • SERVICE

The Queen's Inn, **APPLICATION FOR EMPLOYMENT, page 2**

EMPLOYMENT HISTORY

Give name and address of last two (2) employers, beginning with your present or most recent employer.

❶ Name of Employer: *Hayes Department Store*

Full address (including street, city, state & zip) *845 Midline Street*
Fayetteville, NC 28302

❶ Phone number: *555-543-5365*   Your Supervisor: *Lucy Barnett*

Dates employed (include month and year):   Rate of pay:
FROM: *Sept. 2008*   TO: *present*   STARTING: *$7.25/hr.* ENDING: *$7.50/hr.*

Job Title: *Customer service representative*

Describe your job duties: *I handle returns and exchanges of merchandise. I also receive incoming calls and route them to the correct department. In addition, I am in charge of opening and closing cash registers and training new employees on the registers.*

❷ Reason for leaving: *I would like to pursue my goal of working in hotel management.*

❸ ❷ Name of Employer: _____

Full address (including street, city, state & zip) _____
_____

Phone number: _____   Your Supervisor: _____

Dates employed (include month and year):   Rate of pay:
FROM: _____ TO: _____   STARTING: _____ ENDING: _____

Job Title: _____

Describe your job duties: _____

Reason for leaving: _____

We are an equal opportunity employer and do not discriminate on the basis of age, race, sex, color, religion, or any other basis that is prohibited by law.
I certify that I have completed this application truthfully to the best of my knowledge. I give permission for my previous employers to be contacted. I agree to notify the company if any information on my application should change. In the event that I am hired to work for the company, I understand that any false information given on my application or in my interview will lead to immediate termination from my position.

Applicant Signature: *Clive Robinson*   Date: *9/17/12*

Page 2 of 2

❶ When possible, include phone numbers (with extensions) for your current supervisors. That way, a new employer may dial them directly rather than route through an electronic switchboard.

❷ Clive's reason for leaving ("I would like to pursue my goal of working in hotel management.") helps demonstrate to a potential employer his commitment to a new career in hotel management.

❸ If applicants such as Clive have other previous employers, they should list them here. If not, they should leave this area blank. If applicable, list any relevant volunteer experience in this section.

Sample Application 2

After four years as a carpenter's apprentice, Anu Khosia wants to become a full-fledged carpenter. She holds experience in both residential and commercial carpentry but believes her strength lies on the commercial side. Anu recently spotted a job advertisement for an entry-level commercial carpenter and plans to submit her application (*below*).

1 Any portion of an application that includes the language "Office Use Only" should be completed by the employer rather than by an applicant.

2 Ensure that you follow directions when completing an application. In this case, the employer requests that you **print** all information neatly and legibly.

3 Complete all information to the best of your ability. If you do not have a middle name or initial, simply leave the area blank.

4 Many applications will require you to list whether you've been convicted of a crime. Often, companies also will conduct background checks on candidates. To that end, ensure that you answer all application questions thoroughly and honestly.

ANU • SKILLED TRADE

Date: **March 10, 2012**
JL and Company Construction, LLC

1 Office Use Only
Superintendent: _____
Date of hire: _____

APPLICATION FOR EMPLOYMENT
2 (All information must be printed legibly)

Position Applying for: **Carpenter**

Name: **Khosia** / **Anu** / **3**
Last Name / First Name / Middle Name

Home Address: **118 Hyde Blvd., Apt. 12**

City: **Oregon City** | State: **OR** | Zip Code: **97045**

Home Phone: **(503) 555-1827** | Cell Phone: **(503) 555-1827**

Do you possess a valid driver's license: ☑YES ☐ NO

Highest school grade completed: Circle 1 2 3 4 5 6 7 8 9 10 11 12 (GED)

Name and location of Educational Institution: **Portland Community College**

| Dates of attendance: | FROM | TO **May 2006** |
| Military Service | Branch: | Separation Date: |

4 Criminal Convictions: **none**

Are you a Union Member: ☑YES ☐ NO   ID Number: **5871664**

Have you completed an apprenticeship program: ☑YES ☐ NO Where: Northwest College of Construction

Have you worked for JL and Company in the past: ☐YES ☑ NO   If YES, When:

Work Experience: ☐ Less than 1 Year ☐1-2 Years ☑2-5 Years ☐ over 5 Years

Skill Level: Circle Foreman Leadman Journeyman (Apprentice) Labor

Previous Employers, starting with most recent:

Employer **Standard Commercial Construction**	Employer **R and L Homebuilders, Inc.**	Employer **Building Supply Warehouse**
Job Title **Carpenter's Apprentice**	Job Title **Carpenter's Apprentice**	Job Title **Warehouse Associate**
Dates (Month/Year) **July 2009-present**	Dates (Month/Year) **May 2007-July 2009**	Dates (Month/Year) **August 2006-May 2007**
Supervisor **Joe Bonta**	Supervisor **Derek Redding**	Supervisor **Ken Dahle**
5 Reason for Leaving **Seeking a position as a carpenter**	Reason for Leaving **Accepted construction apprenticeship**	Reason for Leaving **Began carpenter's apprenticeship**

Page 1 of 2

5 When supplying your reason for leaving a position, choose your wording carefully. For example, "Seeking a position as carpenter" sounds more ambitious than "A desire to relocate" or "Divorced and looking for a change."

Sample Application 2, *page 2*

Application for Employment, page 2
JL and Company Construction, LLC

① Describe any safety training you have had.
American Red Cross First Aid and CPR, power tools and pneumatic tools safety training

② **GENERAL JOB DESCRIPTION**

POSITION TITLE: Carpenter, to include all facets of building

REPORTS TO: Project Foreman

ESSENTIAL FUNCTIONS:
Have a good working knowledge of both commercial and residential construction
Comply with all OSHA safety guidelines
Maintain the proper tools of the trade in good working order
Wear proper work attire (work boots, hard hat, and safety glasses)
Report for work on time and prepared

NON-ESSENTIAL FUNCTIONS:
Attend training seminars or other continuing education
Performance of other duties as assigned

MINIMUM QUALIFICATIONS FOR EMPLOYMENT:
All trade positions involve repetitive physical activity
All employees must have the ability to understand and follow instructions in English
Lifting of up to 120 pounds throughout the work day
The daily working environment is uncontrolled

This general job description does not list all the duties of the job. You may be asked by supervisors to perform other duties. You will be evaluated on your ability to perform the tasks set forth in this job description.

③ By signing below I am certifying that I have read and understand this general job description and that the information on this application is truthful and complete. I also understand that any false misrepresentation of myself is grounds for immediate dismissal.

Anu Khosia
Signature

Anu Khosia
Printed Name

Page 2 of 2

① List all professional credentials or certifications that you hold. You also may wish to list any relevant non-credential trainings that you've completed.

② Read each job description carefully and determine whether you have the skills and abilities to perform the specified duties. The requirements in a job description, including related functions and qualifications, will give you a working idea of the types of questions that may arise in an interview.

③ A signed application is a legal document. Therefore, any false statements could lead to disqualification or even termination from a job.

Sample Application 3

Sandra Brown works part-time in the computer services department at the community college at which she received her associate's degree in computer servicing technology. Sandra wants to use her professional experience as well as knowledge and skills from her coursework to advance and become a full-time computer support specialist.

① Some applications will require you to write the job number or job title of the position for which you're applying. Companies—especially *large* companies—use job numbers and titles to help ensure your application routes to the proper department or hiring manager.

② If you've changed your name, such as through marriage or divorce, note your prior name here.

③ Some parts of an application will ask you to check a box rather than to write an answer. Ensure that you only check one of the boxes—the one that applies to you.

④ State honestly a reasonable time frame by which you could start a new position. If you have a job, you first will need to give your current employer appropriate notice—as much as two weeks or more. If you're between jobs, you may be able to start a new one sooner. If you cannot pinpoint a start date, you could simply complete this section by providing a more generic time frame, such as "after July 1."

APPLICATION FOR EMPLOYMENT

Our company is an Equal Opportunity Educational Institution and EEO/Affirmative Action Employer committed to excellence through diversity. Employment offers are made on the basis of qualifications and without regard to race, sex, religion, national or ethnic origin, disability, age, veteran status, or sexual orientation.

<u>PLEASE TYPE OR PRINT</u>. Complete the entire application. You may attach a resume, but you must still complete all questions or your application will be deemed incomplete and may not be considered. Applications with missing or invalid job numbers will not be considered for any position.

Position **①** Applying For: JOB #: 01879	Name (Last, First, Middle): Brown, Sandra, Louise		Other names under which you have attended school or been employed: **②**
Street Address: 6702 Sheridan Avenue	City, State & Zip: St. Louis, MO 63104		
Social Security Number: XXX-XX-XXXX	Home Phone: 314-555-9104	Work Phone: 314-555-0983	Other Phone: 314-555-8445

Are you eligible to work in the United States? **③** ☑YES ☐ NO	
Are you 18 years of age or older? ☑YES ☐ NO	If NO, what is your current age?
If required for position, do you have a valid driver's license? ☑YES ☐ NO	If YES, State of issuance, license #, and expiration date: Missouri, B-2224523, 11/1/2014

Please indicate the days and times you are available to work:
<u>Monday through Friday, daytime and evening hours</u>

④ When are you available to begin working?
<u>Immediately</u>

EDUCATION

Name of School	City/State	Did you graduate?	If NO, # of years left to graduate	If YES, date of Graduation	Degree received	**⑤** Major
College: Centreville Community College	Centreville, MO	☑YES ☐ NO		May 12, 2011	Associate's degree	Computer Servicing Technology
College:		☐YES ☐ NO				

⑤ To some hiring managers, education can be as or more important than experience. This will be especially true if your major, or core area of study, strongly relates to the job for which you're applying.

Sample Application 3, *page 2*

WORK EXPERIENCE

1 May we contact your former employers? ☑YES ☐ NO

Dates Employed (most recent position) FROM: Aug. 14, 2010 TO: May 28, 2011	☐Full time ☑ Part-time If part-time, # hrs./wk: 20	Title: Network Systems Technician I
2 Starting Salary: $9.50/hour Final Salary: $10.50/hour	Organization Name and Address: Centreville Community College 149 Mayweather Way, St. Louis, MO 63101	
Supervisor's Name, Title and Phone #: Jared Seaver, Network Systems Administrator (314) 555-3002		
Primary duties: Assist in maintenance, repair, and installation of network servers, routers, hubs, and switches; systems backups; install and upgrade new system software; maintain user databases		Reason for Leaving: Graduated; seeking full-time employment

Dates Employed FROM: Sept. 12, 2008 TO: Aug. 13, 2010	☐Full time ☑ Part-time If part-time, # hrs./wk: 20	Title: Desktop Support Specialist
Starting Salary: $7.85 Final Salary: $8.65	Organization Name and Address: Centreville Community College 149 Mayweather Way, St. Louis, MO 63101	
Supervisor's Name, Title and Phone #: Nancy Bothell, Desktop Administrator, (314) 555-3015		
Primary duties: Managed campus computers running Windows, Macintosh, and Linux operations systems; assisted students with network setup and access; trained faculty and staff in software use		Reason for Leaving: Promoted

REFERENCES

3 Please complete contact information for three professional references.

Reference Name and Position	**4** Phone Number and Email Address
Jared Seaver, Network Systems Administrator	(314) 555-3002, j.seaver@pax.com
Nancy Bothell, Desktop Administrator, Centreville Community College	(314) 555-3015, n.bothell@pax.com
Professor Margaret Hoff, Chair, Computers and Technology	(314) 555-3145, m.hoff@pax.com

Page 2 of 3

1 The answer to this question almost always should be "Yes." Prospective employers seek to contact previous employers to verify employment and learn more about candidates. However, if you're seeking a job while presently employed at a different company, you may wish to deny a potential employer access to your current employer—since your current employer likely doesn't know of your job search.

2 Starting and ending salary figures can provide a prospective employer with certain insights. For example, they might indicate whether your efforts at a company were valuable enough to merit a pay increase. In addition, they also might give a potential employer a sense of your salary expectations in a new role.

3 This application requests three professional references. Ensure that your professional references are people with or for whom you've worked, whether for pay or on a volunteer basis.

4 Although you want to provide complete and accurate information on an application, you first should check with your references before releasing their contact information. For example, some references may prefer to be contacted by phone. Others may prefer email.

Sample Application 3, *page 3*

1 Ensure that you carefully read the directions on pages such as this one. In this case, Sandra must use a scoring scale of 1 (novice) to 5 (expert), as opposed to simply placing a checkmark next to the programs and applications with which she's most familiar.

2 The directions ask Sandra to omit any operating systems, languages, hardware, or applications that she has never used. However, Sandra should try to fill in as many fields as possible while remaining honest. For example, if Sandra has used a system, language, piece of hardware, or application just once, she could rate it as a "1" instead of leaving it blank.

1 Rate the following operating systems, applications, and programming languages according to your level of expertise, on a scale of 1 to 5. If you have never used any of the following, please leave the field blank. **2**

Novice	Beginner	Intermediate	Advanced	Expert
1	2	3	4	5

OPERATING SYSTEMS	Rating
WINDOWS 2000	5
WINDOWS XP	5
WINDOWS VISTA	4
WINDOWS 7	4
MACINTOSH OS X	4
UNIX	4
LINUX	4
NOVELL NETWARE	4
Other:	

LANGUAGES	Rating
C OR C++	1
SQL	1
HTML	4
VISUAL BASIC	3
JAVA	3
UML	1
Other:	

HARDWARE	Rating
PC	5
MAC	3
PRINTER	4
NETWORK	5
Other:	

APPLICATIONS	Rating
MS WORD 03 (PC)	4
MS WORD 07 (PC)	4
MS EXCEL 03 (PC)	3
MS EXCEL 07 (PC)	3
MS POWERPOINT 03 (PC)	3
MS POWERPOINT 07 (PC)	3
MS PUBLISHER (PC)	3
MS PAGEMAKER (PC)	2
MS ACCESS (PC)	4
MS WORD 08 (MAC)	4
MS EXCEL 08 (MAC)	4
MS POWERPOINT 08 (MAC)	3
MS ACCESS 08 (MAC)	4
OPEN OFFICE	4
DREAMWEAVER	1
FTP OR SFTP	4
SAS	
SPSS	
PHOTOSHOP	
ILLUSTRATOR	
LOTUS NOTES	4
VPN	4
VISIO	2
Other:	

I certify that the information contained in this application is true and accurate.

Applicant Signature: *Sandra Louise Brown*   Date: *June 11, 2011*

Sample Application 4

Throughout his career as an Emergency Medical Technician (EMT), Luis Orazi has earned both his basic and advanced EMT certifications. Now, he hopes to become an EMT supervisor. Luis recently became aware of an opening for a supervisory position within his current company and submitted the employment application below to Human Resources.

LUIS • HEALTHCARE

LIFE CARE EMS
Application for Employment

PLEASE PRINT

PERSONAL INFORMATION

Name: Orazi   Luis   Miguel   Date: November 14, 2012
      (Last)   (First)   (Middle)

Social Security Number: XXX-XX-XXXX

Address: 515 Hanover Street

City: Atmore   State: AL   Zip Code: 36427

Home Telephone Number: 251-555-2991   Are you at least 18 years of age?
Other Phone: 251-555-2867   (YES)   NO

Hours Requested (please circle) (Full Time) Part Time   Date available to Start: 2 weeks from date of hire

How did you find out about this position? Internet posting

Do you have any relatives or friends working here? no

Please list: _____

POSITION INFORMATION

Position(s) Applying For: Emergency Medical Technician Supervisor

Have you ever worked for this organization? Yes

If so, date (s) June 2009-present   Prior Position(s) here: EMT

Reason (s) for leaving Seeking supervisory position within Life Care

CERTIFICATION INFORMATION
(List only current certifications - photocopies required at interview)

Certification	Certification Number	Expiration Date	Certifying Agency
CPR			
EMT/EMT-P (circle one)		May 10, 2013	American Red Cross
National Registry	P7473729		
PALS		June 8, 2012	ACLS Training Center
ACLS		March 5, 2012	ACLS Training Center
BTLS		March 5, 2012	ACLS Training Center
EMD		Jan. 12, 2013	ACLS Training Center
CDL		Feb. 22, 2014	State of Alabama
Other: _____			

1 You want to have as many points of contact on an application—home and cell phone numbers and email and street addresses—so that company officials easily may reach you.

2 Some companies are very large, with hundreds or even thousands of employees. An employee who previously worked for a given company, provided he or she left on good terms, may be viewed positively by current hiring officials.

Page 1 of 6

3 This application requires Luis to only list current certifications required for this position. Note that Luis must produce a photocopy of the certification(s) at the time of an interview, so it will benefit him to answer honestly.

Sample Application 4, *page 2*

WORK REQUIREMENTS AND GENERAL INFORMATION

Can you provide proof, if hired, that you are eligible to work in the U.S.? (YES) NO
Do you have a valid Driver's License? (YES) NO   Class D

Issued by what State? _Alabama_   Driver's License #: _O-24919305305_
List all moving violations (convictions) and accidents and any suspensions or revocations of your license in the last five years: _Speeding ticket, August 2007_

Have you ever been convicted, or pled guilty or no contest to a felony or misdemeanor, including a DUI/DWI or similar offense, had any moving violations, or had your license revoked or suspended?   YES (NO)
If yes, explain:_____

❶ **A conviction will not necessarily disqualify you from employment.**
Have you ever been excluded or are you currently excluded from participating in any federal health program such as Medicare or Medicaid?   YES (NO)
If yes, explain:_____

EMPLOYMENT HISTORY
❷ (List your last three employers or volunteer activities, starting with the most recent.)

I.

Employer: _Life Care Ambulance Service_
Job Title: _Emergency Medical Technician_   Supervisor: _Kathy Donovan_
Start Date: _June 18, 2009_   Salary: _$24,960_
❸ End Date: _Presently employed_   Salary: _$26,450_
Job Description (including duties and responsibilities): _Ambulance driver and first responder. Assess patients in the field and provide advanced triage treatment; communicate with doctors and nurses regarding treatment and transfer; checking of medical equipment, vehicles, and tools._
Employer's Telephone #: _251-555-8943_   May we contact? (YES) NO

Reason for leaving: _To work as an Emergency Medical Technician Supervisor_

❶ This application states that a conviction will not necessarily disqualify an applicant from employment. If you have a conviction, use this area to explain ways in which you learned from the experience.

❷ When listing employment, begin with your most recent job, then your next most recent, and so on. The employer's application may provide more or fewer fields than you need. If you need to list additional employment, you can use the back of an application page. If you have less experience, you can leave extra areas unfilled.

❸ Employers tend to favor candidates who are presently employed over those who are between jobs. They view employed candidates as more current with their skills and abilities than those who have been out of the workforce.

Sample Application 4, *page 3*

LUIS • HEALTHCARE

EMPLOYMENT HISTORY
(List your last three employers or volunteer activities, starting with the most recent.)

II.

Employer: _Rabun Volunteer Fire Department_

Job Title: _Volunteer Firefighter_   Supervisor: _Edward Brown_

Start Date: _March 2008_   Salary: _Volunteer_

End Date: _June, 2009_   Salary: _____

Job Description (including duties and responsibilities): _Responsible for all duties of a_ _firefighter for small volunteer department: checking and maintenance of_ _vehicles and equipment; fire management, search, and rescue; public_ _education_

Employer's Telephone #: _251-555-0001_   May we contact? (YES) NO

Reason for leaving: _Completed basic EMT training and began working full-time_

PAST EMPLOYMENT

Have you ever been:

❶ Disciplined or terminated for reckless driving?   YES (NO)

Placed on probation or terminated for excessive absenteeism?   YES (NO)

Disciplined or fired for insubordination?   YES (NO)

Disciplined or fired for violation of safety rules?   YES (NO)

Disciplined or fired for assault or fighting?   YES (NO)

Disciplined or fired for harassment?   YES (NO)

Disciplined or fired for patient abuse?   YES (NO)

Disciplined or fired for alcohol- or drug-related activity at work?   YES (NO)

❷ If you answered yes to any question above, please explain: _____

_____

Answers of Yes for any of the above questions will not necessarily disqualify you from employment.

❶ Carefully read and honestly answer each question. Keep in mind that your prospective employer may conduct a background check. To that end, you'll want to ensure that you've been honest about any issues that might influence their hiring decision, such as whether you've ever been disciplined or terminated by an employer.

Page 3 of 6

❷ Take advantage of the opportunity to explain from your perspective the reasons for any past discipline by employers.

Sample Application 4, *page 4*

EDUCATION AND TRAINING

HIGH SCHOOL:

Name: _Andalusia High School_   Address: _1380 Watertown Way_

Years completed: _____   _Andalusia, AL 36420_

❶ Did you graduate? (YES) NO   If not, highest grade completed: _____

Did you receive your GED?   YES (NO)

COLLEGE:

Name: _____   Address: _____

Years completed: _____   _____

Did you graduate?   YES   NO   If not, highest year completed: _____

Degree: _____   Major: _____

TECHNICAL SCHOOL:

Name: _Lurleen B. Wallace State Jr. College_   Address: _Andalusia, AL_

Years completed: _1_ _____   _____

Did you graduate? (YES) NO   If not, highest year completed: _____

Certificate: _EMT–basic and advanced_   License: _____

❷ Expires: _May 2013_   Expires: _____

EMS/FIRE SERVICE RELATED TRAINING NOT LISTED ABOVE: _____

_____

_____

EMS/FIRE/PROFESSIONAL AFFILIATIONS (other than listed under prior employment):

_____

_____

❶ In this area, note your high school educational outcome. Did you graduate with a diploma or earn a GED credential? If not, what was the highest grade that you completed?

❷ Some certifications and licenses expire. If you hold a professional certification or license, include its date of expiration, if applicable.

Sample Application 4, *page 5*

REFERENCES

1 List **three** persons, other than relatives, who have knowledge of your work experience and/or education.

Name: Edward Brown   Address: 3162 Pearl Street

Occupation: Fire Chief - Rabun VFP   Minette, AL 36507

2 Years Known: 3   Telephone: 251-555-0001
(including area code)

Name: Kathy Donovan   Address: 325 West Bassette Ave.

Occupation: EMT supervisor   Mobile, AL 35508

Years Known: 2   Telephone: 251-555-8943
(including area code)

Name: Randy Pickett   Address: 1000 Dannelly Blvd.

Occupation: Instructor   Andalusia, AL 36420

Years Known: 3   Telephone: 251-555-2602
(including area code)

3 List **two** personal references that have known you for at least three years outside work.

Name: Chelsea MacArthur   Address: 5672 Dauphin St.

How they know you: Friend through church   Mobile, AL 36608

Years Known: 5   Telephone: 251-555-8734
(including area code)

Name: Shane Hudson   Address: 254 Schillinger Rd.

How they know you: Friend since high school   Mobile, AL 36608

Years Known: 10   Telephone: 251-555-1276
(including area code)

1 At some point, you may have worked for a relative in a family business. Try to avoid including a relative as a reference, since he or she may be less objective than someone with whom you had a strictly professional relationship.

2 Try to cite references with whom you worked for at least one year. That way, they can speak to your skills and abilities across a span of time.

3 Personal references should be friends who can attest to your character. For example, are you reliable? Dedicated? Willing to take on extra responsibility?

4 Page 5 of 6

4 As you can see, this application includes greater detail than either of the previous two. Still, ensure that you complete all aspects of the application.

Sample Application 4, *page 6*

1 For an application to be considered an official document, an applicant must sign and date it. By virtue of his or her signature, an applicant attests to the accuracy of the information contained within the application.

ACKNOWLEDGEMENT

I certify that all information given in this application is true to the best of my knowledge. I understand that any information found to be false may be grounds for dismissal, if hired.

1 Applicant's Signature: *Luis Miguel Orazi*   Date: *November 14, 2012*

Printed Name: *Luis Miguel Orazi*

FOR OFFICE USE ONLY:

LIFE CARE EMS

2900 34th Street
Atmore, AL 36427
(251) 555-8900

Sample Application 5

As you've seen, the length of employment applications can vary depending on the requirements set by each organization. Jacinda Hernandez, an educator with many years of experience, wants to become an assistant professor at a university. Although Jacinda has an extensive work history, her employment application only requires two pages.

JACINDA • EDUCATION

PAXEN STATE UNIVERSITY

APPLICATION FOR EMPLOYMENT

Name: Jacinda   M.   Hernandez
First   MI   Last

Other names by which you have been known:
For date verification and reference checking purposes   Jacinda Romero

Address: 1861 Hyacinth Street
Street / Route / PO Box

City: Calabasas   State: CA   Zip: 91302

Phone: Home (818) 555-6250   Work (818) 555-2290

Position which you are currently applying for: Assistant Professor in Educational Leadership

NOTICE OF INTENT TO COLLECT PRIVATE DATA

All applicants are asked to provide the data in this application for the purpose of processing your application. State employees who perform personnel or payroll functions and search committees may have access to the data, provided their work reasonably requires access. Others who have legal access to the data may include: Legislative Auditor, Attorney General, enforcement agencies with statutory authority, and any other person or entity authorized by law or court order.

POST-SECONDARY EDUCATION (list all degrees):

Institution/State	Degree	Date Earned	Major(s)	Specialty (if any)
Univ. of California, LA	Ed. D	May 2006	Educational Leadership	ELL
Univ. of California, LA	M.A.	May 2002	Ed. Leadership, Admin	ELL
Univ. of the Pacific	B.S.	May 1996	Elementary Education	ELL certification

Employment History—Please list your most recent employer first. If applicable, include volunteer work and self employment. Provide an explanation for any gaps in employment. All information in this section must be complete. A Curriculum Vitae should be attached. Please attach additional pages if necessary.

1. Employer: Los Angeles Unified School District

Address: 333 S. Beaudry Ave., Los Angeles, CA 90017   Phone: (213) 241-2600

Starting Job Title: ESL/ELL Program Coordinator | Final Job Title: ESL/ELL Program Coordinator

Supervisor's Name and Title: Albert Vanderwal, Superintendent

Dates of Employment:
FROM (month/year): August 2006 TO (month/year): present

Job Duties: Design, implement, and coordinate ESL/ELL programming; assess individual school programs and provide feedback; organize teacher training; select curriculum; evaluate teacher effectiveness

Reason for Leaving: To use my education and experience to teach at the university level.

Page 1 of 2

1 Jacinda's specialty involves teaching courses in English Language Learning, or ELL. If she were applying for a professorship in an ELL department (as opposed to the Department of Educational Leadership), she would want to add more detail to the category *Specialty*. For example, instead of listing "ELL" under *Specialty*, Jacinda might wish to list "ELL Reading."

2 Some companies may use shorter applications and request that you also submit a resume. In Jacinda's case, she will need to submit a Curriculum Vitae (CV) along with her application. As you'll see in Chapter 2, a curriculum vitae is more detailed than a resume. Those seeking academic jobs at colleges or universities use CVs rather than resumes.

3 If attaching additional pages, such as those for a CV, ensure that you include on each page your name, the name of the position, and any relevant job code. That way, if your application materials were to become separated, an employer would be able to easily reassemble them.

Sample Application 5, *page 2*

① Try to maximize the available space on applications to fully convey your qualifications for the position.

② In this case, the employer requests that applicants attach references or reference letters to their application. Applicants should seek to comply with this and other similar requests, since such references likely will give their candidacies an extra boost.

2. Employer: Los Angeles Unified School District
Address: 333 S. Beaudry Ave., Los Angeles, CA 90017 **Phone:** (213) 555-2600
Starting Job Title: Itinerant ESL Teacher | **Final Job Title:** Itinerant ESL Teacher
Supervisor's Name and Title: Margo Hamilton
Dates of Employment:
FROM (month/year): August 2003 **TO (month/year):** May 2006
① **Job Duties:** Provided ELL support in elementary classrooms; tutored students individually; visited schools on a rotating basis; planned and delivered professional-development sessions.
Reason for Leaving: Became ESL Program Coordinator upon completion of Ed.D.

3. Employer: San Luis Coastal School District
Address: 1500 Lizzie Street, San Luis Obispo, CA 93401 **Phone:** (805) 555-1200
Starting Job Title: Itinerant ESL Teacher | **Final Job Title:** Itinerant ESL Teacher
Supervisor's Name and Title: Adam Howard
Dates of Employment:
FROM (month/year): April 2002 **TO (month/year):** August 2003
Job Duties: Provided individualized English Language Learner support, especially with reading skills
Reason for Leaving: Moved to a new district

REFERENCES
② Please provide references or reference letters as indicated in the Notice of Vacancy (attach sheet)

Are you legally eligible to work in the United States? ☑YES ☐ NO

PLEASE CAREFULLY READ THE FOLLOWING STATEMENTS
③ **Authorization to Release Information:** By my signature, I consent to the release of information (including but not limited to information concerning my past and present work performance; including my official personnel files; attendance records, evaluations, and educational records including transcripts; military service; law enforcement records; and/or any personnel record deemed necessary) from other entities to Paxen State University.
Signature: *Jacinda M. Hernandez* **Date:** February 6, 2012

Certification of Applicant: By my signature, I affirm, agree, and understand that all statements on this form are true and accurate. Any misrepresentation, falsification, or material omission of information or data on this application may result in exclusion from further consideration, or, if hired, termination of employment. I have requested herein that my present employer not be contacted. An offer of employment may be conditioned upon acceptable information and verification from such employer prior to beginning work.
Signature: *Jacinda M. Hernandez* **Date:** February 6, 2012

Page 2 of 2

③ Rather than requiring an applicant to provide information listed in the area **Authorization to Release Information**, the school wants Jacinda's signed permission that the school may request and receive copies of her records from previous employers and schools.

Delivering Your Application

If you decide to hand-deliver your application, use it as an opportunity to make a good first impression. If you're lucky, a hiring manager might be available to interview you on the spot—so be prepared with supporting documentation (*see box to the right*). After you've delivered your application, follow up a week later by phone to check on its status.

DRESSING FOR SUCCESS

Hiring experts say you never get a second chance to make a first impression. With that in mind, following are strategies to make the most of a first appearance with potential employers:

Dress appropriately for your potential work environment. Men should wear a dress shirt and slacks. Women should wear the same or a business-appropriate dress.

Make-up should be appropriate for the job.

Cover any tattoos with clothing.

If you plan to meet with a potential employer, ensure that you style your hair appropriately to the job for which you're applying.

As a rule of thumb, men should match the color of their shoes and belt to their slacks.

Wear appropriate footwear for your profession. Heels of reasonable height are appropriate for women. Closed-toe shoes other than sneakers are recommended.

LESSON REVIEW

▶ Assessment

1. Describe the purpose of a job application.

2. Describe the importance of closely following instructions when completing a job application.

3. A basic job application requires a candidate to provide what forms of information?

4. Why do employers require applicants to sign and date applications?

5. What steps should a candidate take to ensure he or she makes a strong first impression with hiring officials?

Online Job Applications

TERMS

employment profile

track

search engine

kiosk

references

You can shop online, read news articles online, and even watch TV series and movies online. You now also can apply for jobs online. The Internet has changed the way people seek and apply for jobs. Many companies have their own Web sites on which you can search and apply for jobs. In addition, there are several sites, such as Monster.com, on which you can search for jobs and even upload your resume for hiring managers to see and review.

There are several advantages to applying for jobs online. For example, some sites enable you to register and build an online employment profile. An **employment profile** contains much of the same information—contact numbers and work and education histories—as your resume. You then can set your profile to receive email alerts when the company adds new jobs to its site. That way, you can apply for specific jobs quickly. In addition, many of these sites allow you to **track**, or follow, jobs for which you've applied. This eliminates the uncertainty that often comes with the job-seeking process. It also enables you to check the status of your application at any time.

ACTIVITY

▶ Untangling the Web

For job seekers, the Internet can be a web of confusion, with a dizzying number of employment sites. Large online sites such as *Monster.com* and *CareerBuilder.com* list thousands of positions.

However, lesser-known sites also may help job seekers to identify opportunities. Examine the sites below and on the next page. Then think about ways to use them in your job search.

Search the Company Name and "Jobs"
Use a search engine, such as Google. Type in a company's name (one in which you have interest), and then add a *.jobs* extension to it. That will route you directly to information about jobs at a given company.

Searching Online

Companies typically use simple and familiar Web addresses so that they may be found easily on the Internet. Often, a Web address includes the company's name, followed by .com (which stands for *commercial* businesses). Many addresses, such as *www.walmart.com* and *www.target.com*, take you directly to company Web sites.

Some companies, however, may have more complicated online addresses. For example, a pizza restaurant in California uses *sonnys.com* as its Web address.

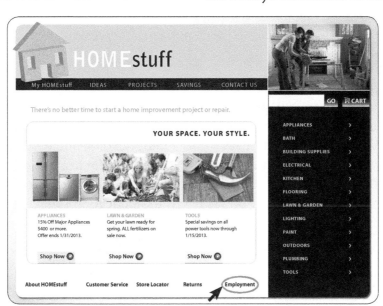

Company Web sites, such as this one, include links to career opportunities. Here, candidates may use the "Employment" link to find and apply for positions.

Another restaurant, the southern chain Sonny's Bar-B-Q, uses the address *sonnysbbq.com*. The Sonny's restaurant in California secured its Web address first, leading the southern chain to customize its online address to avoid confusion between the two.

If you cannot find a company by using its name and *.com*, then type its name and location into a search engine. A **search engine**, such as Google, Bing or Yahoo, is a type of software application used to locate documents and Web sites online.

Visit snagajob.com
This Web site lists hourly positions available in your area. Simply enter your zip code and then narrow your search by company and location. Create an account with *snagajob* to apply for any of its listed jobs.

Visit LinkUp.com
You also can visit meta-sites such as LinkUp (*www.linkup.com*), a search engine that lists job openings from a variety of company Web sites. LinkUp allows job seekers to search by company, city, or zip code.

Applying for Jobs Online

Company Web sites can be a main source of job listings. Often, these sites include the most up-to-date information on a given company. When searching for jobs, you should investigate sections of the site called "Careers," "Employment Opportunities," "Jobs" or even "About Us."

Most company sites list all available jobs. These may include both part-time and full-time and hourly and salaried jobs. A company's Web site will provide information about each job, its necessary skills, and the instructions for applying for it. A companion online applicant-tracking system, or ATS, typically requires the same information as does a paper application.

This includes your contact information, educational background, and employment history. You may be asked the dates and wages of previous jobs and the days and times that you are available to work. You should have this information available when you apply for jobs.

As with hard-copy applications, ensure that you proofread and edit your electronic application before submitting it. In the editing process, you'll want to add certain keywords from the posting and remove errors. Some hiring officials may eliminate candidates for a single error in an application. Lastly, by submitting online you can ensure that your application routes directly to hiring officials.

❶ Many companies have a link to jobs from their home page. At this Web site, for example, you would click on "Job Opportunities."

❷ Sites such as this one provide a full listing of open positions. You simply click on one of the job titles to receive more information— salary, qualifications, and so on—about it.

❸ Some company Web sites include an RSS (Real Simple Syndication) feed, which is a place where you can sign up for email alerts about jobs. If not, frequently check the Web sites of companies at which you would like to work for new job listings.

Kiosk Applications

Some companies have hiring kiosks in their stores or offices. Some of these **kiosks**, or small and open structures, are free-standing. Other kiosks are at desks with computers. You can complete job applications at these kiosks, so plan to bring everything you'll need to finalize your application. For example, you should have a copy of your resume and work history, including names of and contact information for previous employers. You may wish to put printed information in a folder for increased organization and privacy.

The application at a hiring kiosk most likely will be specific to that store or company. It also can be specific to a certain job. For example, if you are applying for a job as a clerk, the questions likely will be specific to that job. If you instead wish to apply for a job as a driver, an interviewer likely will ask you about your driving experience. The kiosk will guide you through the process of completing an application. Read and answer each question fully before moving to the next one. Hiring managers can review applications from a hiring kiosk immediately, which makes the hiring process more efficient for them—and you.

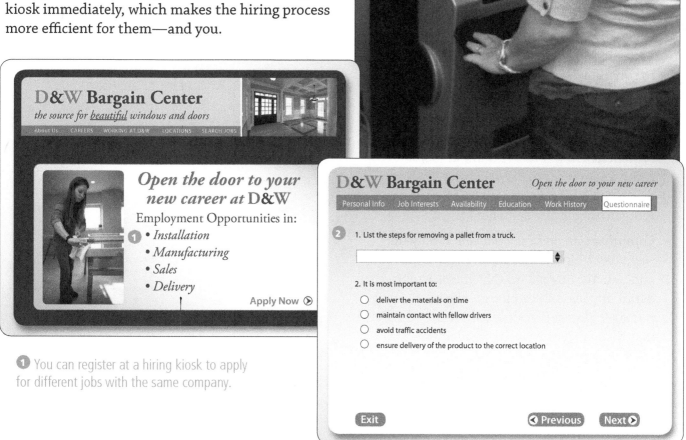

D&W Bargain Center
the source for <u>beautiful</u> windows and doors

About Us   CAREERS   WORKING AT D&W   LOCATIONS   SEARCH JOBS

Open the door to your new career at **D&W**

Employment Opportunities in:
❶ • *Installation*
• *Manufacturing*
• *Sales*
• *Delivery*

Apply Now ⊙

D&W Bargain Center   *Open the door to your new career*

Personal Info   Job Interests   Availability   Education   Work History   Questionnaire

❷   1. List the steps for removing a pallet from a truck.

⬍

2. It is most important to:

○ deliver the materials on time
○ maintain contact with fellow drivers
○ avoid traffic accidents
○ ensure delivery of the product to the correct location

Exit   ◐ Previous   Next ◑

❶ You can register at a hiring kiosk to apply for different jobs with the same company.

❷ As part of the application process, a kiosk program may pose questions designed to measure your knowledge of the position.

Check Your Application

You always should review your application before submitting it. A paper application allows you to review everything in hard-copy form, which may make it easier to spot errors. With an electronic application, however, you may only see a small piece of it—such as one screen—at a time.

Still, you should check your online application as you move through it. In most cases, you will be able to move forward and backward through your application prior to submitting it. However, in some cases you may not be able to go back and make changes. Therefore, you should check information in each section before moving to the next one. Remember to check for:

- *Spelling*. If you are unsure about how to spell a word, use a program such as Microsoft Word to run a spell check. If you are at a hiring kiosk and lack access to a spell-check program, use a simpler word in place of the tougher one.

- *Grammar*. Ensure that you write clear sentences using correct grammar. If you think a sentence sounds incorrect, then try to rewrite it by substituting certain words or reorganizing entire sentences.

- *Capitalization and Punctuation*. It may not seem like a big deal, but correct capitalization and punctuation shows that you're attentive to detail. If you don't catch such errors, a hiring manager almost certainly will! If they do, they may disqualify you from consideration for the position.

Remember to check all parts of your application before submitting it. Your goal: to produce a professional-looking, error-free document that promotes your candidacy by selling your skills, education, and experience to hiring managers.

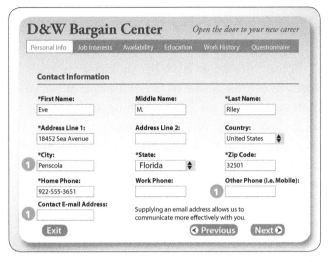

1 Eve misspelled *Pensacola* and did not list additional contact information, such as an email address, which can make it difficult for an employer to reach a candidate.

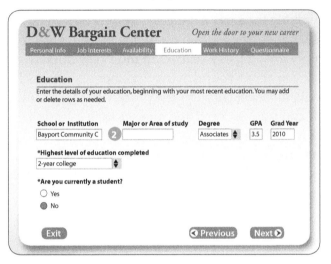

2 Here, Eve failed to enter her major area of study in school. A college major can provide potential employers with important information about a candidate.

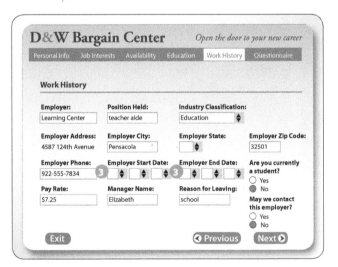

3 Eve omitted her start and end dates for this job. On some sites, these may be required fields, meaning one cannot submit the application without completing them.

Online Employment Tests

For some jobs or companies, you will be required to take a pre-employment test. These tests also may be called talent assessments or career tests. They help an employer learn whether you will be a good fit for their company or a specific job. A pre-employment test may test you for specific skills. For example, if you want to become a nurse, a pre-employment skills exam will test you for skills related to the nursing field. In many cases, you will take this test along with your online application. An employer will use your test results to help determine whether to call you for an interview. Some questions may be multiple-choice while others may be open-ended. The following questions will serve as a guide to those you may encounter on a pre-employment test. Read those questions and respond to them in the spaces below.

Before Gwen could start her nursing job at the hospital, she had to take a pre-employment exam to assess her nursing skills.

▶ Sample Questions

1. A customer has complained about the same problem three times. What should you do?

   A. ask her to explain the problem and tell her that you'll resolve it

   B. ensure that the employee who helped her the last time will help her again this time

   C. request that she wait while you talk to the last person she talked to and find out why it hasn't been resolved

   D. refer her to your manager, who hopefully will resolve the issue

2. Do you prefer to work alone or in a group? Explain.

   _____

   _____

   _____

3. Do you make a list before going to the grocery store or walk through each aisle to find those items you need? Explain.

   _____

   _____

   _____

   _____

4. Think of a time in which you experienced conflict. How did you resolve it? What types of strategies did you use?

   _____

   _____

   _____

LESSON REVIEW

▶ Assessment

1. Describe ways in which to navigate the Internet for job listings.

2. Identify and describe an advantage in creating an employment profile and uploading your resume to a company's Web site.

3. Why should you review application materials before submitting them?

4. What purpose do pre-employment tests serve?

NWTC Library
2740 W. Mason St.
Green Bay, WI 54307

Pathways

Steps to a Successful Submission

▶ 1. Read the application

Skim the application to learn the type—and amount of information—the company wants.

For example, each job application will require you to provide some of the same information, such as your name, street address, and phone number(s). In general, an application will require you to provide information across three categories:

- **Education:** Schools, colleges, or universities you've attended, along with the diploma or degree you received and the grade-point average you attained

- **Work history:** Names of businesses, dates of employment, range of responsibilities, supervisors' names, contact information, and reason for leaving a position

- **Military service:** Dates of service and date and type of discharge

You should compile this information before applying for jobs. That way, you can simply copy the information over to your job application without the need to memorize names, dates, and locations. You'll also be less likely to omit information.

▶ 2. Fill out the application

Ensure that you complete all fields, especially those that include a star or asterisk (*) next to them. Such symbols indicate required fields. In some cases, an applicant-tracking system (ATS) may allow you to upload a resume or cover letter. If they do, ensure that you customize these materials to each position for which you apply.

Depending on the ATS, you may be able to provide general, rather than specific, information for areas such as salary. You instead could use the word *negotiable*, which would suggest to an employer your willingness to compromise on salary.

▶ 3. List references

Many job applications will ask for a list of references. These **references**, or individuals who can speak to your ability to perform a particular job, should attest to your skills and abilities relative to the position for which you've applied. References may be personal and professional. They can include friends, current or former co-workers, and even teachers.

When compiling references, you should store each name and contact—including phone number and email address—in an electronic or paper file for easy storage and retrieval. You then should organize references according to each position for which you're applying. For example, if you're applying for clerical positions that require knowledge of a certain type of software, you'll want references who can speak to your mastery of those systems.

▶ 4. Review and submit

After you've completed the application, you then should proofread it for errors. Employers often require your signature on the application to verify that you've given accurate information. With electronic applications, this often involves clicking a button on the site prior to submission.

As you review your application, keep in mind that it should include these three features:

- **Neatness.** Write or type legibly to ensure understanding. Messy or illegible writing can leave an employer with the impression that you lack attention to detail. Some employers may discard an application rather than try to decipher it.

- **Completeness.** Enter information thoroughly, especially for required fields.

- **Accuracy.** Double-check all information to ensure its accuracy. Employers can disqualify candidates or fire employees for lack of honesty on applications.

Chapter Recap

Using the list below, place a checkmark next to the goals you achieved in Chapter 1.

▶ **In Lesson 1, you . . .**

- ☐ Learned the purpose of a job application
- ☐ Understood the importance of following directions on an application
- ☐ Analyzed how to complete and submit a job application

▶ **In Lesson 2, you . . .**

- ☐ Learned to use the Internet to seek and apply for jobs
- ☐ Understood the importance of reading and revising an application
- ☐ Examined the role of pre-employment tests

Chapter Review

CHAPTER 1

Name: _____ Date: _____

▶ **Directions:** Match the terms in the left column to the correct definition in the right column.

_____ 1. employment profile

_____ 2. applicant-tracking system

_____ 3. search engine

_____ 4. job application

A. an online database that collects, stores, and even ranks applicant information

B. a type of software application used to locate documents and Web sites online

C. an online applicant summary that includes much of the same information as a resume

D. a print or electronic form that potential employees must complete to be considered by a company for employment

▶ **Directions:** Choose the best answer.

5. Mandatory fields in job applications often are indicated by the presence of

   A. yellow highlights.

   B. stars or asterisks.

   C. exclamation points.

   D. red circles.

6. Which of the following techniques could a job seeker use to find and apply for opportunities online?

   A. navigate to a specific company's Web site

   B. visit an online employment site such as *Monster.com*

   C. use a kiosk program

   D. all of the above

▶ **Directions:** Determine whether the following statements are true or false. If the statement is true, write T. If the statement is false, write F. Then rewrite the false statement to make it true.

7. You should dress and act professionally when delivering an employment application.

_____

_____

8. Applications at kiosks tend to be very general in nature.

_____

_____

▶ **Directions:** Write your answer to the question on the lines below.

9. Why would candidates want to track online the positions for which they've applied?

_____

_____

_____

10. What are some similar requirements for job applications?

_____

_____

_____

11. Describe how you could use the Internet to seek and apply for jobs.

_____

_____

_____

_____

_____

12. List and describe the process involved in the successful completion of a job application.

_____

_____

_____

_____

_____

Name: _____   Date: _____

▶ **Directions:** Review and complete the sample job application below.

13.   Page 1 of 2

APPLICATION FOR EMPLOYMENT
(All information must be printed legibly)

PERSONAL		
	Date:	
Name:	Home Phone:	
Address:	Cell Phone:	
City:	State:	Zip:
Job applying for:	Job status applying for: ☐ Full Time ☐ Part Time ☐Temporary	
When are you available to begin work?		
Are you legally eligible to be employed in the United States? ☐YES ☐ NO		
Are you over the age of 18 years? ☐YES ☐ NO		
What hours/days are you available to work?	Do you plan to keep your current job? ☐YES ☐ NO	
Do you have friends or relatives working for our company? ☐YES ☐ NO		
Have you ever been convicted of a crime? ☐YES ☐ NO If YES, Explain.		
Have you ever been terminated from a job? ☐YES ☐ NO Why?		
Do you have reliable transportation? ☐YES ☐ NO		

EDUCATION & TRAINING			
	High School	College(s)	Technical School(s)
Name of School:			
Address of School:			
Years completed:	☐1 ☐2 ☐3 ☐4	☐1 ☐2 ☐3 ☐4 ☐5 ☐6	☐1 ☐2 ☐3 ☐4

SKILLS
Please describe any specialized training, and/or skills you have had:

APPLICATION FOR EMPLOYMENT, page 2

EMPLOYMENT HISTORY

Give name and address of last two (2) employers, beginning with your present or most recent employer.

❶ Name of Employer: _____

Full address (including street, city, state & zip)   _____

_____

Phone number: _____   Your Supervisor: _____

Dates employed (include month and year):   Rate of pay:
FROM: _____ TO: _____   STARTING: _____ ENDING: _____

Job Title: _____

Describe your job duties: _____

_____

_____

Reason for leaving: _____

❷ Name of Employer: _____

Full address (including street, city, state & zip)   _____

_____

Phone number: _____   Your Supervisor: _____

Dates employed (include month and year):   Rate of pay:
FROM: _____ TO: _____   STARTING: _____ ENDING: _____

Job Title: _____

Describe your job duties: _____

Reason for leaving: _____

We are an equal opportunity employer and do not discriminate on the basis of age, race, sex, color, religion, or any other basis that is prohibited by law.
I certify that I have completed this application truthfully to the best of my knowledge. I give permission for my previous employers to be contacted. I agree to notify the company if any information on my application should change. In the event that I am hired to work for the company, I understand that any false information given on my application or in my interview will lead to immediate termination from my position.

Applicant Signature: _____ Date: _____

Resumes

Chapter Recap	Chapter Review
☑ ————	————
☑ ————	————
☑ ————	————

Resume Components

GOALS

EXAMINE resume components . . 34-55

LEARN ways to incorporate each component into your resume 34-55

TERMS

resume

objective statement

qualifications

work experience

education, training, certification

vocational training

In Chapter 1, you learned that nearly everyone who applies for a position must complete an application of some variety. In many cases, especially those involving candidates who are seeking professional positions, job seekers also must submit a resume as part of their application. A **resume** is a career summary that describes an applicant's education, skills, work history, and expertise in relation to a specific job posting.

Often, a resume provides the best tool by which to advertise and market your talents. Because such talents vary from one person to another, so do resumes. Regardless of a candidate's background, however, an effective resume typically contains the same component parts. As you can see in the sample resume on p. 35, a standard structure includes the following components: *Contact Information*; *Objective*; *Qualifications*; *Work Experience*; *Education, Training, Certifications*; and *Achievements/Awards*. Some resumes may include more or less information in a given area, such as *Work Experience*, depending on an applicant's level of professional experience.

A resume provides an applicant with a tool for marketing his or her talents and qualifications to potential employers.

Carter Finley
8342 Jefferson Street
South Euclid, OH 44121

cfinley@pax.com
(216) 555-0328

OBJECTIVE:

To bring my graphic design talents to a dynamic, creative graphic design team in a marketing or advertising agency.

QUALIFICATIONS:

Creative graphic designer with four years of experience designing content-rich web sites. Skilled in *Illustrator, Photoshop, Flash, InDesign, Dreamweaver, HTML, CSS*, and *PHP*.

WORK EXPERIENCE:

2007-2011   *Web Content Developer*, Newark Advocate, Newark, OH
Create web pages and graphic content for various clients.

EDUCATION, TRAINING, CERTIFICATIONS:

2011   *Associate of Applied Science Degree (AAS) in Digital Media Design Technology*
Central Ohio Technical College, Newark, OH 43055

ACHIEVEMENTS/AWARDS:

Best Animation Award – Central Ohio Technical College
Spring Exhibition, 2010

Resumes vary in length according to an applicant's level of experience. For example, those newer to the workforce, like Carter (left), may be able to convey their expertise in a single page. Others with more experience may require an additional page.

In this chapter, you'll learn about resume components and ways in which to customize them to a particular industry or opening. In addition, you'll learn how to combine components and use strategies from the chapter to form a well-crafted resume.

For starters, a well-written resume should relate closely to the position for which, and the company at which, you're applying. You'll want to write your resume on a computer using a word-processing application, such as Microsoft Word. If you lack access to a computer, you instead may opt to use a professional resume-writing service.

You'll want to produce two versions of your resume—a plain-text resume and a formatted resume. A plain-text resume lacks formatting, which makes it ideal for electronic submissions. Electronic applicant-tracking systems scan plain-text resumes for keywords.

In contrast, a formatted resume should include easy-to-read fonts, such as Arial, Times New-Roman, or Verdana, avoid fancy design treatments, and run one or two pages in length. When complete, you'll want to save your resume to a hard drive and possibly to a second source, such as a thumb drive.

Upon completion, your resume should be polished, professional, and error-free. You should plan to customize your resume to each position for which you're applying. If possible, you should seek to include in your resume specialized language, such as keywords, from the job posting. Although very few people are hired solely on the strength of their resume, a poor resume can eliminate candidates from consideration. In contrast, a well-written resume like yours should entice a hiring official to contact you about the next stage in the hiring process, the interview.

Contact Information

The first component in your resume, your contact information, should be clearly visible at the top of your resume. Ensure that your points of contact, including your land line and/or cell phone numbers and street and email addresses, are current and correct. If not, hiring officials may discard your candidacy in favor of those applicants they can quickly reach.

For your contact information, use the complete name by which you're commonly known (*Mike* or *Michael*). If you have a common last name, such as *Jones* or *Smith*, you may wish to use a middle initial (*Michael T. Jones*). If possible, you should include a home address. If you are between homes, you should use a post-office box address.

If you intend to list an email address as a point of contact, ensure that you have a professional-sounding account (*MichaelTJones@hotmail.com* rather than *MikeLoves2Party@hotmail.com*). You may register for free accounts through services such as Hotmail and Gmail. If you have a Web resume or an ePortfolio, you also may wish to list that Web address in your contact information.

There are many ways to format and display contact information on a resume. Examine the different formats below and on the next page for ideas about how to format your contact information. For more information, type in the keywords *resume formatting contact information* in your favorite Internet search engine.

CLIVE • SERVICE

Clive T. Robinson

7254 Ashland Avenue ◆ Raeford, NC 28376 ◆ 555-543-7504 ◆ Clive.Robinson@pax.net

❶ Clive centered his contact information at the top of his resume, placing his name (including his middle initial) in a larger point size and boldfaced font so that it will stand out. The rest of Clive's contact information appears beneath his name in a smaller, lightfaced font with symbols to separate portions of his contact information.

ANU • SKILLED TRADE

Anu Khosia

118 Hyde Blvd., Apt 12
Oregon City, Oregon 97045
(503) 555–1827, AnuK@pax.com

❷ Anu's contact information also appears at the top of her resume, but on the far right side rather than at the center. Like Clive, Anu's name appears in bold type. However, Anu has set the point size for her name just slightly larger than the rest of her contact information. Anu, who has a more distinctive last name than Clive, did not see the need to include a middle initial as part of her name.

SANDRA • INFORMATION TECHNOLOGY

❸ **SANDRA L. BROWN** *6702 Sheridan Ave, St. Louis, MO 63104 ◆ (314) 555-9104 ◆ slbrown@pax.com*

❸ Sandra decided to use a single-line format for all of her contact information. Her name appears in bold, capital letters and at a much larger point size than the rest of her information. Like Clive, Sandra chose to use her middle initial and a symbol to separate portions of her contact information.

LUIS • HEALTHCARE

❹ **Luis M. Orazi**
515 Hanover St., Atmore, AL 36427
h: 251-555-2991 c: 251-555-2867
l.orazi@pax.com

❹ Like Anu, Luis justified his contact information to one side (left) rather than to the middle. Luis' name appears in a boldfaced font and at a slightly larger point size than the rest of his contact information. Luis also listed both home (h:) and cell (c:) phone numbers. By listing his home phone number first, Luis signals that employers should first try to contact him at that number and use the cell number as a backup.

JACINDA • EDUCATION

Jacinda M. Hernandez, Ed.D.
1861 Hyacinth Street, Calabasas, CA 91302
(818) 555-6250
jhernandez@pax.com

❺ Jacinda centered and separated her contact information across four lines. Her name appears at a slightly larger point size than the rest of her information.

Objective Statement

On your resume, an **objective statement** summarizes for an employer your skills and career goals. An objective statement runs about one to three sentences (a brief paragraph) in length and appears beneath your contact information. An objective statement may be known by other names *(see box, right)*. You should customize your objective statement for each opportunity for which you apply. Try to limit your use of the word *I* since it may suggest to a hiring official that you're more interested in helping yourself than the company.

Your work experience—or lack thereof—will factor into your approach for writing an objective statement. Candidates with little or no professional experience, such as Clive and Anu, should indicate in their objective statement an openness to learning new skills. Those with significant experience, such as Jacinda, also should exhibit a willingness to learn, while likewise promoting their abilities and achievements. Ideally, those abilities and achievements should relate to and align with the position for which they're applying.

ALSO KNOWN AS ...

Goal
Career Goal
Interest
Job Target
Career Objective

CLIVE • SERVICE

❶ INTEREST

To leverage my superior customer-service skills and begin a career in hotel management as a front-desk clerk.

❶ Clive uses the heading "Interest" for his objective statement. Clive's objective statement concisely explains his willingness and enthusiasm to apply his customer-service skills to a new career field, hotel management.

ANU • SKILLED TRADE

❷ Career Goal

To use and further develop my carpentry skills by working as a carpenter for a commercial firm.

❷ Anu, who uses the words "Career Goal" to headline her objective statement, describes her desire to further develop her carpentry skills through a new opportunity. Employers tend to positively view candidates who are open to continuing education and training.

SANDRA • INFORMATION TECHNOLOGY

③ Job Target To work as an internal technical support team member, bringing my skills in database management and system administration software, as well as installation, maintenance, and repair of desktop and network hardware, to a new and challenging position.

③ Sandra's objective statement, referred to as a "Job Target," runs longer than either Clive's or Anu's. In it, Sandra details specific skills she possesses and would bring to a new position.

LUIS • HEALTHCARE

④ Objective

To work as an Emergency Medical Technician (EMT) supervisor, bringing my personal and professional skills to a challenging work environment.

④ Luis' objective statement communicates his chosen career and the skills, both personal and professional, that he would bring to a new opportunity.

JACINDA • EDUCATION

⑤ CAREER OBJECTIVE: A skilled and qualified educational leader with years of teaching and leadership experience who seeks to use acquired knowledge and expertise to positively impact a college or university through effective organization, communication, and leadership.

⑤ Jacinda's objective statement briefly summarizes for a potential employer her vast skills and experience and how both would transfer to a new role.

Qualifications Section

Whereas objective statements state a candidate's goals *(To work as an internal technical support team member...)*, a **qualifications** section summarizes in a brief paragraph a candidate's most impressive skills, abilities, and achievements as they relate to an opportunity. In short, qualifications statements—also known as summaries of qualifications and by a variety of other names *(see box, right)*—target employer needs rather than the individual goals that objective statements do.

A well-written qualifications summary features strong, active verbs, such as *directed* and *developed*, that show employers the key role(s) you played in a particular effort or achievement. Because hiring officials only spend an average of 10 to 20 seconds reviewing a resume, applicants must get—and keep—their attention. In the example that follows, the applicant does just that by outlining duties, quantifying achievements *(monthly savings, consistent promotions)*, and providing information about certification and his or her chosen career path *(all noted below in blue underline)*. In addition, note the use of active verbs *(directed, managed, streamlined, awarded, earned)* throughout the qualifications summary below *(all noted in red underline)*.

ALSO KNOWN AS ...

Overview

Strengths

Career Summary

Professional Overview

Professional Background

Executive Summary

Expertise

Summary of Qualifications

Highlights of Qualifications

- Directed solar cell installation, photovoltaics, and retrofitting of old and new structures for energy efficiency.
- Managed group of solar cell installers, providing direction and feedback on performance annually and at other times throughout the year.
- Streamlined operational procedures, resulting in $2,500 monthly savings for company.
- Awarded consistent promotions to positions of increased responsibility.
- Earned green energy star certification

A strong qualifications section lists a candidate's skills, abilities, and achievements. If applying for a position as a solar panel installer, for example, a candidate should include information about his or her experience in installation, photovoltaics, and/or retrofitting.

A strong qualifications summary also includes various keywords, or those words specific to your skills, job title, experience, training, and degree. Ideally, keywords in your resume should match those in the job posting, since applicant-tracking systems and hiring managers will scan for them. Keywords enable hiring managers to quickly identify an applicant's qualifications. If your resume includes certain keywords, you may advance to a phone or an in-person interview. If it lacks them, however, you may be eliminated from consideration.

To the right you can see two qualifications summaries. Notice the difference? The second summary, which includes keywords (*underlined in blue*), provides more specific information, which can help an employer better understand a candidate's strengths and value to the company. Below and on the pages that follow, you'll see many ways in which to format the qualifications section of your resume. As you review the *Qualifications* sections for Clive, Anu, Sandra, Luis, and Jacinda, please note the various terms they used in their qualifications summaries. Also note the active verbs and keywords for each job seeker.

1. Goal-oriented with 10 years of experience and a strong ability to meet client needs and expand growth.

2. Goal-oriented marketing professional with a 10-year proven track record in product innovation. Practiced in market research and analysis, developing product launch and promotion strategies, and providing product marketing and mapping.

A strong qualifications section can help propel candidates past the resume phase and on to an interview.

CLIVE • SERVICE

STRENGTHS

Customer Service
- Possess strong communication skills that result in unsurpassed customer service
- Persevere to resolve challenging issues
- Return customer calls promptly and courteously
- Manage customers, provide reassurance, and resolve conflict

Office and Technical
- Understand POS cash register systems, hardware, and software
- Direct the opening and closing of cash registers
- Operate various pieces of office equipment
- Answer and direct customer calls on multi-line phone systems

❶ Since Clive lacks extensive work experience, he uses the term "Strengths" to emphasize his qualifications rather than his limited employment history.

❷ Clive organizes his skills into two categories, **Customer Service** and **Office and Technical**. He then highlights strengths that match the position he hopes to secure.

Qualifications Section

Your qualifications summary may be the only section of your resume that a hiring manager reads. For that very reason, you should word your summary clearly, concisely, and convincingly.

As you can see in Anu's example below, an applicant may use targeted phrasing in a summary, such as "skilled carpenter" or "demonstrated ability" to promote his or her candidacy.

❶ Career Summary

❷ Certified and skilled carpenter with 4 years of apprentice experience in residential and commercial construction and with vast knowledge of building codes. Experienced in framing, trim, doors, cabinets, stairs, roofing, and sheetrock, steel framing, and wooden concrete forms. Demonstrated ability to work in a team environment. Highly attentive to detail and deadlines.

❶ Anu used the term "Career Summary" to head her qualifications section. She wrote a brief overview of her experience, skills, and accomplishments targeted to the job for which she's applying.

❷ Anu included in her career summary the following keywords tailored to the job for which she's applying: *residential and commercial construction*, *building codes*, *framing*, *trim*, *doors*, *cabinets*, *stairs*, *roofing*, *sheetrock*, *steel framing*, *wooden concrete forms*, *team environment*, and *deadlines*.

The use of targeted words or phrases in a qualifications summary can help get, and keep, a hiring manager's attention. For example, Anu cited in her summary for a commercial carpentry position words such as "certified," "experienced," and "attentive," which help quickly convey her skills and expertise to a hiring manager.

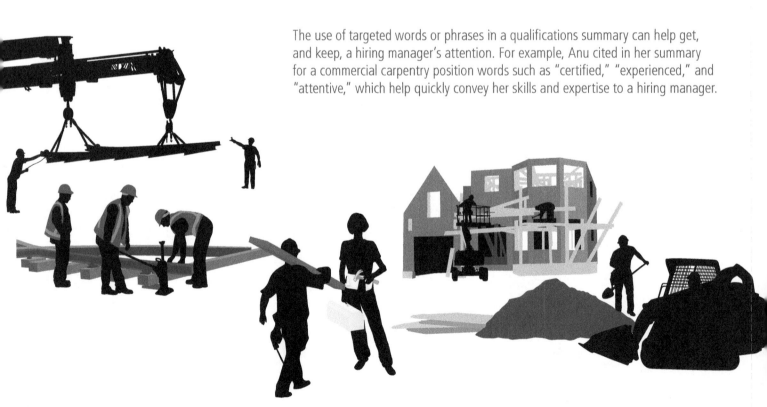

Because each position will have its own set of requirements, you should seek to customize your summary for each job for which you apply. First, you should carefully read each job description.

Next, you should identify the most important qualifications in each description. Finally, as you write your qualifications summary, you should attempt to mirror those requirements and terms.

SANDRA • INFORMATION TECHNOLOGY

① **Overview** **②** Network Systems Technician/IT Specialist with 4+ years of experience with network administration and maintenance, system backups, databases, hardware and software for Windows, Macintosh, and Linux operating systems.

① Sandra used the term "Overview" to highlight her qualifications in a brief paragraph.

② In the Overview section, Sandra spotlighted her experience, including her knowledge of various computer operating systems.

Think of your qualifications summary as an elevator pitch. For example, imagine you're in an elevator with a potential employer with 10 seconds to convince that person to hire you. What would you say? Next, put that pitch in writing as a qualifications summary.

Qualifications Section

Hiring managers may receive dozens or even hundreds of resumes for a single job opening. How can they review all of them? For starters, they only spend a few seconds reviewing each resume.

In that time, they discard most candidates and only contact a few for interviews. Those lucky few possess well-crafted summaries that incorporate keywords, active verbs, and targeted phrasing.

LUIS • HEALTHCARE

① Professional Background

② Superior skills as an Emergency Medical Technician, responding to a variety of emergency calls in an urban environment

- Alabama State EMT advanced certification and valid motor vehicle operator's license with excellent driving record
- National Registry of Emergency Medical Technicians certification
- American Red Cross Professional Rescuer
- Physical and mental ability to work in a challenging emergency medical environment, to think critically, and to use independent judgment in routine and non-routine situations
- Excellent communication and interpersonal skills that combine to produce and maintain strong relationships with management, fellow EMTs, and volunteers
- Ability to take direction, follow instructions carefully, and delegate

① Luis headlines his qualifications summary with the title "Professional Background."

② Luis uses an introductory paragraph followed by bullets to showcase his qualifications. This format enables a hiring manager to scan his resume for keywords and relevant experience.

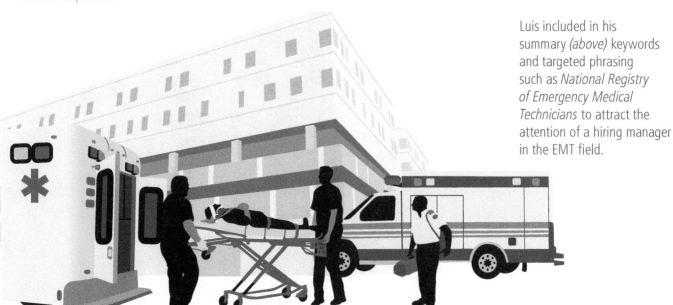

Luis included in his summary *(above)* keywords and targeted phrasing such as *National Registry of Emergency Medical Technicians* to attract the attention of a hiring manager in the EMT field.

After you've written a qualifications summary, you should review it to ensure accuracy and to eliminate typographical and other errors. You also could have friends or family members review it.

Hiring officials expect to receive error-free submissions from candidates. Even the smallest issue on a resume could lead a hiring official to eliminate a candidate from consideration.

JACINDA • EDUCATION

① PROFESSIONAL OVERVIEW—EDUCATIONAL LEADERSHIP

② More than 20 years of experience in education

- ESL/ELL program coordination
- Direct support of classroom teachers
- Teacher staff development

- One-on-one work with students
- Classroom teaching experience
- ESL paraprofessional experience

① Jacinda included the words "Educational Leadership" to fully describe her professional experience and to help position her for a high-ranking position in the field of education.

② As with Luis, Jacinda chose to include her areas of expertise in a bulleted list for ease of reading and review.

Jacinda hopes to use her background in ESL/ELL teaching to secure a job in higher education.

Work Experience

For many candidates, a qualifications summary provides an opportunity to frame and hopefully optimize their professional achievements. In many respects, it represents the sizzle of a candidate's resume. Employers, however, find the steak in the section on **work experience**, in which they can see at a glance the positions you've held, the duties and responsibilities you've fulfilled, and any honors or promotions you've earned. The work experience section of your resume should extend and enrich the skills and abilities you outlined in the qualifications section. It may be known by other names *(see box, right)*.

Most resumes use a reserve-chronological format, in which candidates list their most recent position—including, if it applies, their current position—first, followed by the next most recent position, and so on. For each position, you'll want to add beginning and ending employment dates (by year and by month) next to or beneath each job title, followed by a summary of your duties and responsibilities.

As with your qualifications section, you'll want to begin each work experience entry with active verbs. If you're describing current duties, you should use present-tense verbs (e.g., *perform, assemble, transport*). If you're describing prior responsibilities, you should use past-tense verbs (e.g., *performed, assembled, transported*).

ALSO KNOWN AS ...

Employment Experience
Work History
Relevant Experience
Related Employment
Professional Experience
Employment Summary
History
Professional History
Business Experience
Employment Record
Career History

As a customer service representative, Clive works closely with shoppers. You can see his employment experience on the next page.

Of all the components that together comprise your resume, the work experience section likely will be the lengthiest. To that end, please use these strategies to help shape and refine your efforts:

- *List all of your experience.* On a sheet of paper, brainstorm and list your current and past jobs and responsibilities. Ensure that you include in your list both volunteer and paid positions. For now, concentrate on placing your thoughts on paper. You can edit your material later.

- *Organize your experience.* Group your experience by industry, function, and date. For example, if you're seeking a position in the healthcare field, first organize all of your experience in that industry. Next, group it according to function (e.g., nursing). Finally, list it by date, beginning with your current or most recent position and working backward.

- *Choose the most relevant experience.* Describe your most relevant experience for each position for which you're applying and its alignment to your career objective. For example, if you're applying for a job in customer service, you may wish to list both your communication and computer skills. However, you may opt to list your communication skills first since they may align better with your stated career objective.

- *Prioritize your experience proportionately.* Regardless of whether you produce a 1- or 2-page resume, you'll have limited space in which to describe your combined experience. As such, you'll need to determine the proper amount of space for each job entry. You may opt to use more space to describe your most recent or a highly relevant position and less to describe a distant and/or less relevant position. For example, if you were applying in the area of information technology, you may find your knowledge of computer systems to be useful. If you were applying in the field of nursing, however, you may not.

- *List your work experience in brief paragraphs and bullet points.* Short paragraphs and bulleted lists enable employers to quickly scan resumes for relevant keywords and experience. Hiring officials may ignore or discard resumes with lengthy paragraphs.

- *Review, edit, and revise.* As you finalize the work experience portion of your resume, review and revise it to eliminate any unnecessary words and to correct any typographical errors. You may wish to print and edit your work experience document by hand and then type any changes into your document file.

CLIVE • SERVICE

EMPLOYMENT EXPERIENCE

① **Customer Service Representative,**   3/2008 to Present
Hayes Department Store, Fayetteville, NC

② Customer service position receiving and routing calls to appropriate departments, handling returns and exchanges, assisting with cash register training and troubleshooting, and ensuring customer satisfaction.

① Clive, a cashier at a local department store, lists his title as a customer service representative because he believes it will better help qualify him for the position he wants as a front-desk clerk.

② Clive lists the duties he performed on this job, some of which go beyond the scope of a normal customer service representative, such as training. Ensure that you list all the duties you perform at a job, especially if they exceed the scope of your title. Such additional responsibilities show hiring managers you can multitask and take on extra work.

Work Experience

Those newer to the workforce may struggle to fulfill experience requirements in job postings. For example, a carpenter's position may require 1-to-3 years of relevant experience as an apprentice.

Although candidates with less experience may be considered with the right mix of education and experience, they should seek to enrich their resumes by citing freelance or volunteer efforts.

Work History

① *Carpenter's Apprentice*   Standard Commercial Construction, Hillsboro, OR   2009–2011
- Built commercial office and retail buildings
  - Involved in all aspects of the building process from start to finish
- Built wooden concrete forms
- Worked on steel framing crew
- Experience with building codes for commercial buildings

② *Carpenter's Apprentice*   R and L Homebuilders, Inc., Hillsboro, OR   2007–2009
- Worked on various projects from start to finish, including new residential homes, additions, and remodels
  - **②** Experienced in framing, trim, doors, cabinet installation, stairs, roofing, and sheetrock
- Competent with all hand tools and air tools used in typical carpentry

Warehouse Associate   Building Supply Warehouse, Beaverton, OR   2006–2007
- Operated forklift in loading and unloading lumber inventory
- Operated horizontal band saw, cut-off saw, and banding machine
- Pulled and shipped lumber product orders to stores

① Anu lists her title (in italic font, so that it stands out), company name, and dates of employment in her work history.

② Anu bullets her duties and responsibilities for easy navigation and reading. She also includes sub-bullets, in the form of dashes, that further detail her duties.

Anu's work history indicates an increase in responsibility from Warehouse Associate to Carpenter's Apprentice.

In contrast, candidates with vast experience may face a different challenge: keeping resumes to two pages. In that case and as a rule of thumb, you should list your three most recent positions.

Older positions may be grouped together using a category such as *Other Professional Experience*— *Nine years as customer-service professional in automotive, retail, and insurance industries.*

SANDRA • INFORMATION TECHNOLOGY

❶ Relevant Experience

Network Systems Technician I
August 2010 – May 2011

Centreville Community College
Centreville, MO

Challenge: To ensure a smooth transition for faculty and staff to new software on all campus computers

Action: Interviewed faculty and staff to assess their level of knowledge of the new systems. Based on this information, prioritized the information to be conveyed to staff before, during, and after the transition. Provided faculty and staff with several weeks' notice and a specific timeline of the transition. Wrote and distributed a handbook that simplified use of the new system, including troubleshooting tips.

Results:
- A reduction in the number of calls and complaints from faculty and staff compared to the previous software upgrades
- Commendations from faculty and staff on the process, as well as the ease of use of the manual and the new system
- Personal recognition from the software consultants on a smooth transition

Desktop Support Specialist
September 2008 – August 2010

Centreville Community College
Centreville, MO

❷ Challenge: To develop and implement a systematic process to answer student queries on network setup and access, software installation and use, and printing issues

Action: Developed a survey for students to identify their computing needs and areas in which they need the greatest assistance. The survey asked students to rate the current computer services so that inefficiencies could be assessed. Designed a process by which students can send their queries via email and receive a reply, providing them with a time frame by which to expect answers. In addition, designed and implemented an online schedule for students to meet one-on-one with computer support staff.

Results:
- A reduction in the number of calls and complaints from faculty and staff compared to the previous software upgrades
- Commendations from faculty and staff on the process, as well as the ease of use of the manual and the new system
- Personal recognition from the software consultants on a smooth transition

❶ Here, Sandra highlights experience that directly relates to the job for which she's applying. She even uses the term "Relevant Experience" to headline this section of her resume.

❷ Because Sandra wants to transition to a more demanding position, she uses a format that emphasizes prior challenges she faced, actions she took, and results she achieved.

Work Experience

Much like your career objective should reflect your professional goals, your current and past experiences must showcase that you're the best candidate for the job for which you're applying.

When listing your current and past professional experiences, emphasize those responsibilities that indicate you're qualified to take the next step in your career, as Luis did below.

Related Employment

Emergency Medical Technician, Mobile, AL   June 2009 to Present ❶
❷ • Perform patient assessment and provide advanced triage treatment

• Operate a variety of medical devices and equipment following approved treatment protocols

• Exchange information with nurses and doctors in the Emergency Room as well as between EMTs on incoming and outgoing shifts

• Check medical equipment, vehicles, and tools to ensure working order

Voluntary Firefighter, Rabun, AL   March 2008 to June 2009
• Maintained emergency vehicles such as fire trucks and ambulances

• Delivered public safety education

• Member of search-and-rescue and fire management operations teams

❶ By using the words "June 2009 to Present" and present-tense verbs to describe his duties, Luis conveys to potential employers that he's currently employed as an EMT.

❷ Luis' diverse duties, including his efforts in triage and emergency room treatment and as a volunteer firefighter, suggest to an employer that he may be ready for a supervisory role.

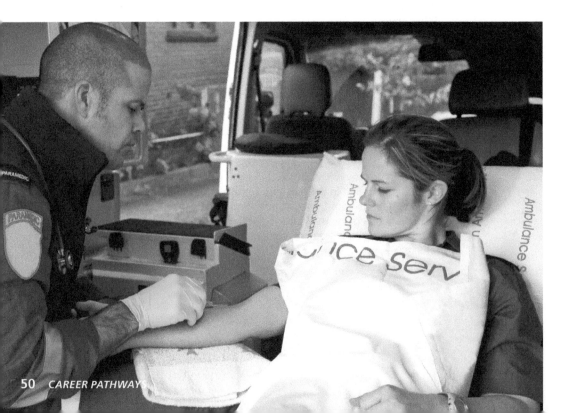

Luis hopes to leverage his experience as an EMT into a supervisory position.

As noted previously, hiring officials prefer resumes that list work experience entries in reverse-chronological order. This allows officials to quickly take note of a candidate's qualifications.

Jacinda intends to apply for a very competitive position as an assistant professor. She lists her work experience in reverse-chronological order, with very detailed descriptions for each entry.

JACINDA • EDUCATION

PROFESSIONAL EXPERIENCE

1 **Los Angeles Unified School District (LAUSD), Los Angeles, CA**

ESL/ELL Program Coordinator (2006 to Present)
Design, implement, and coordinate ESL/ELL programming for LAUSD
Assess individual school programs and provided feedback. Organize ESL/ELL teacher training.
Achievement(s):
- Improved scores in reading and mathematics for all ESL/ELL learners in LAUSD over a 4-year period.

Itinerant ESL Teacher (2003 to 2006)
Provided ESL support in elementary classrooms; worked with individual students on reading and writing skills
Achievement(s):
- Reduced classroom discipline issues
- Increased integration of non-English speaking and English-speaking students
- Improved scores in reading and mathematics

San Luis Obispo School District, San Luis Obispo, CA

Itinerant ESL Teacher (2002 to 2003)
ESL/Reading Resource Teacher (1999 to 2002)
Provided ELL support in elementary classrooms; worked with individual students on reading and writing skills
Achievement(s):
- Improved scores in reading and mathematics
- Improved reading and writing skills

Elementary Teacher (1996 to 1998) **2**
Taught 3rd and 4th grade students in all subjects. Assisted in training of ESL/ELL paraprofessionals.
Achievement(s):
- All students showed progress in all subjects
- Developed training curriculum for ESL/ELL paraprofessionals

ESL Paraprofessional (1988 to 1992)
Assisted classroom teachers with English-language learning students. Instructed small groups of ESL/ELL students. Aided students in understanding and completing of assignments.
Achievement(s):
- Helped students achieve a homework completion rate of 90%

1 Jacinda underlined her places of employment so that they would stand out from other areas of her professional experience.

2 Here, Jacinda has a one-year gap in employment between her position as an elementary teacher (ending in 1998) and her role as an ESL/Reading resource teacher. Jacinda should be prepared to discuss the gap in an interview setting.

Education, Training, Certification

If done properly, your resume should tell employers a story. For example, your objective statement, qualifications summary, and work experience should align with and support one another. The section that follows your work experience—**education, training, and certification**—should do the same. Ideally, your education, training, and certification should include information, such as major courses of study and degrees, that support your career decision. For example, if you're pursuing a position in information technology (IT), you should have a degree and possibly experience in computer science.

Along with traditional high school or college educations, many people seek **vocational training**, or training in a particular industry or position. Sometimes, vocational training leads to professional certification. Many professions, from plumbers to construction workers and on through graphic designers, may require workers to pass and hold professional certifications. Below and on the next page, please review the education, training, and certification sections for Clive, Anu, Sandra, Luis, and Jacinda.

ALSO KNOWN AS ...

Credentials
Certification
Licenses
Training
Professional Development
Continuing Education

CLIVE • SERVICE

EDUCATION

Sandhills Community College, Pinehurst, NC
1 • 15 hours of coursework toward a degree in business management
  • High School diploma, Fayetteville (N.C.) High School

1 Although Clive hasn't yet completed his business management degree, he still lists it on his resume to demonstrate to an employer his ongoing interest and dedication.

ANU • SKILLED TRADE

2
Technical Licenses and Certifications

• Carpenter's Certification, Northwest College of Construction, Portland, OR	2011
• GED credential, Portland Community College, Portland OR	2006

2 Anu lists both her GED and carpentry certifications, which convey to an employer Anu's ability to complete her high school education and to seek additional, trade-specific schooling.

Spotlight relevant certifications or licenses, including any trainings you've attended. List schools you've attended and from which you've graduated, beginning with the most recent.

In general, limit education entries on your resume to high school and beyond. In general, hiring officials only will be interested in your level of education most relevant to the job posting.

Education

Centreville Community College, Centreville, MO 63633
- Associate's Degree in Computer Servicing Technology (AAS)
- ❸ Grade-point average (GPA) 3.75

❸ In general, you should plan to include your grade-point average (GPA) only if it's 3.0 or higher. In this case, Sandra lists her GPA of. 3.75. High GPAs can help candidates, especially recent graduates who lack significant professional experience.

Technical Certifications and Degrees

Lurleen B. Wallace State Jr. College, Andalusia, AL
- ❹ EMT—Advanced, 2011
- EMT—Basic, 2009

❹ Luis lists both of his completed training programs—EMT Basic and EMT Advanced. If you received two or more degrees, certifications, or licenses from the same institution, you can include them in a bulleted list under the institution's name, as Luis does here.

EDUCATION AND CREDENTIALS

❺ **Ed.D., Educational Leadership,** "An Analysis of ELL Program Integration: Examining Shared Traits of Successful Implementations," University of California, Los Angeles, 2006
M.A., Education, Educational Leadership and Administration, University of California, Los Angeles, 2002
B.S., Elementary Education, ELL Certification, University of the Pacific, 1996

❺ Jacinda's series of college degrees tells a powerful story about her commitment to the field of education. She first earned an undergraduate degree in elementary education, followed by advanced degrees in education and then educational leadership.

Achievements/Awards

Most resumes close with a section about achievements and awards. These entries should tie into and help support the story you're telling, through your resume, to hiring officials. You should list in order, from most recent to most distant, any achievements you've realized or awards you've earned in your career. As you can see below, strong achievements should include hard data that drives a hiring official to action.

ACHIEVEMENT STATEMENTS

Weak Statements	Strong Statements
Helped the company to grow	Increased company profits by 23%
Trained project team	Developed training series that increased project efficiency by 30%
Fielded customer calls	Implemented client-retention model that reduced cancellations by 25%

Lastly, you may provide references to employers later in the process and in a separate file or on a separate sheet of paper. For now, you may note references on your resume as "Available upon request."

CLIVE • SERVICE

AWARDS

❶ Employee of the Year,
Hayes Department Store   2010-2011

❶ Try to limit awards to those relevant to the job for which you're applying. Clive's award for employee of the year helps highlight his value to a hiring manager as a dedicated employee.

ANU • SKILLED TRADE

❷ Memberships

- Member, United Brotherhood of Carpenters and Joiners of America
- Member, Northwest Regional Council of Carpenters

❷ Anu lacked work-related achievements or awards, so she instead opted to spotlight her work-related memberships, which help demonstrate her dedication to the carpentry field.

Achievements	• *Integration of new system software.* ❸ Directed campus-wide integration of new computer system software, resulting in an on-time delivery schedule. • *Lead trainer.* Trained campus faculty and staff in the use of computer systems and software, resulting in a time savings of 6 hours per employee.

❸ When listing your achievements, use active verbs that help promote the significance of your contribution to your employer.

❹ Leadership Recognition

2011 recipient of the Outstanding Team Member Award for Leadership; Selected for prestigious EMT Accelerated Leadership Development Supervisor Training Program

❹ To help bolster his application for a supervisory position, Luis highlights the leadership recognition award that he recently received.

❺ AWARDS

| 2006 | *Dean's Scholar Award*, UCLA Graduate School of Education & Information Studies |
| 2004 | *Educational Administration Scholarship*, American Association of School Administrators |

❺ Jacinda, who wants to work in higher education, emphasizes her university academic honors.

LESSON REVIEW

▶ Assessment

1. What are the standard resume components?

2. Write an objective statement for your resume.

3. Why are keywords important to include in a resume?

4. What is the purpose of the *qualifications* section of a resume?

5. Why would a candidate seek to include achievements and awards in a resume?

6. How does the *qualifications* section differ from the *achievements* section of a resume?

Resume Formats

GOALS

LEARN the purpose of various resume formats
. 56–63

EXAMINE the role of a curriculum vitae
. . . . 61–63

UNDERSTAND the importance of resume formatting
. 64–65

TERMS

format

skills resume

reverse-chronological

hybrid resume

curriculum vitae

When it comes to resumes, beauty often is in the eye of the beholder. Strong resumes include the components discussed in Lesson 1: *Contact Information*; *Objective*; *Qualifications*; *Work Experience*; *Education, Training, Certifications*; and *Achievements/ Awards*. Although resumes largely include the same components, their **format**, or the way in which they present resume content, may vary.

Each format provides candidates with a unique look and style. Candidates should use criteria such as their level of experience or education to select a format. The formats themselves will vary according to factors such as:

- the nature or amount of content in each component
- the sequence of categories or subcategories
- the use of common styles, such as margins, leading (the spacing between lines of text), and font and point size

Four of the most common formats include the skills resume, the reverse-chronological resume, the hybrid resume, and the curriculum vitae (VEE • tay). Each format enables candidates to present their professional qualifications in the best possible light. The table below lists each format, its features, and the candidates who would stand to benefit the most from its use.

Candidates will seek to select a resume format that optimizes their professional qualifications.

MAIN RESUME FORMATS

This format ...	... highlights ...	... for ...
Skills resume	qualifications, skills, and abilities	those new to the workforce or those with a gap in their employment history
Reverse-chronological	work experience	candidates with a lengthy work history
Hybrid resume	skills and work experience combined	those candidates with strong skills and work experience
Curriculum vitae	academic and scientific honors	candidates with strong academic accomplishments

Skills Resume

A **skills resume** emphasizes candidates' strengths and skills rather than their experience. In general, a skills resume benefits candidates:

- newer to the workforce
- changing careers
- seeking to re-enter the workforce

As you can see, Clive uses a skills resume to list his many customer service and technical strengths.

In concept, a skills format will draw a hiring manager's attention to a candidate's skills, rather than to his or her level or lack of experience. In practice, however, hiring officials understand well the purpose behind skills resumes. For that reason, hiring managers sometimes tend to consider less seriously those candidates who use a skills resume. Still, though, for many they continue to be a viable resume option.

Clive T. Robinson

7254 Ashland Avenue ◆ Raeford, NC 28376 ◆ 555-543-7504 ◆ Clive.Robinson@pax.net

---

❶ Customer Service/Hospitality Specialist
**Customer Service • POS System Specialist • Office Management
Telephone Reception • Computer Systems**

INTEREST

To leverage my superior customer-service skills and begin a career in hotel management as a front-desk clerk.

❷ STRENGTHS

Customer Service
- Possess strong communication skills that result in unsurpassed customer service
- Persevere to resolve challenging issues
- Return customer calls promptly and courteously
- Manage customers, provide reassurance, and resolve conflict

Office and Technical
- Understand POS cash register systems, hardware, and software
- Direct the opening and closing of cash registers
- Operate various pieces of office equipment
- Answer and direct customer calls on multi-line phone systems

EDUCATION

**Sandhills Community College,
Pinehurst, NC**
- 15 hours of coursework toward a degree in business management
- High School diploma, Fayetteville (N.C.) High School

EMPLOYMENT EXPERIENCE

Customer Service Representative,   3/2008 to Present
Hayes Department Store, Fayetteville, NC

Customer service position receiving and routing calls to appropriate departments, handling returns and exchanges, assisting with cash register training and troubleshooting, and ensuring customer satisfaction.

AWARDS

Employee of the Year,   2010-2011
Hayes Department Store

❶ Although he lacks direct experience in the hospitality field, Clive highlights his applicable customer-service and technical skills.

❷ Clive lists his professional skills and abilities under the qualifications section titled "Strengths"—prior to his education and work experience sections. Clive also reverses the traditional order of employment experience followed by education, in an effort to boost his business background.

Reverse-Chronological Resume

Unlike the skills resume, hiring managers favor the reverse-chronological resume. A **reverse-chronological** resume emphasizes a candidate's employment experience and achievements by first listing the most recent (or current) position, then the next most recent, and so on. Candidates who use this format often include a qualifications summary as well as dates of employment for their various positions. These dates of employment should be organized both by year and by month and in a way that hopefully shows little or no gap between jobs.

1 Sandra lists in her reverse-chronological resume both a job target (qualifications summary) and an overview (objective). In the best resumes, the overview section aligns with and supports the job target, as Sandra's does.

2 Under each job title, you should list your duties and responsibilities for that position. Here, Sandra uses a **Challenge-Action-Results** format to describe her responsibilities, outline key efforts, and explain the outcomes she achieved.

SANDRA L. BROWN 6702 Sheridan Ave, St. Louis, MO 63104 ◆ (314) 555-9104 ◆ slbrown@pax.com

1 Job Target

To work as an internal technical support team member, bringing my skills in database management and system administration software, as well as installation, maintenance, and repair of desktop and network hardware, to a new and challenging position.

1 Overview

Network Systems Technician/IT Specialist with 4+ years of experience with network administration and maintenance, system backups, databases, hardware and software for Windows, Macintosh, and Linux operating systems.

Relevant Experience

Network Systems Technician I   Centreville Community College
August 2010 – May 2011   Centreville, MO

2

Challenge: To ensure a smooth transition for faculty and staff to new software on all campus computers

Action: Interviewed faculty and staff to assess their level of knowledge of the new systems. Based on this information, prioritized the information to be conveyed to staff before, during, and after the transition. Provided faculty and staff with several weeks' notice and a specific timeline of the transition. Wrote and distributed a handbook that simplified use of the new system, including troubleshooting tips.

Results:
- A reduction in the number of calls and complaints from faculty and staff compared to the previous software upgrades
- Commendations from faculty and staff on the process, as well as the ease of use of the manual and the new system
- Personal recognition from the software consultants on a smooth transition

Page 1 of 2

Reverse-Chronological Resume, *page 2*

Each work experience entry should begin with an active verb (e.g., *interviewed, developed*) that briefly but clearly states your responsibilities for that position. As possible, you also should include results produced by your efforts. Those results should be both specific and measurable. Increased traffic at a Web site that you developed or higher sales figures that you delivered are two examples of specific and measurable results. In some cases, especially among recent graduates, candidates may list their educational histories before their employment histories.

SANDRA L. BROWN ❸   **Page 2**
(314) 555-9104 ◆ slbrown@pax.com

Desktop Support Specialist	Centreville Community College
September 2008 – August 2010	Centreville, MO

Challenge: To develop and implement a systematic process to answer student queries on network setup and access, software installation and use, and printing issues

Action: Developed a survey for students to identify their computing needs and areas in which they need the greatest assistance. The survey asked students to rate the current computer services so that inefficiencies could be assessed. Designed a process by which students can send their queries via email and receive a reply, providing them with a time frame by which to expect answers. In addition, designed and implemented an online schedule for students to meet one-on-one with computer support staff.

Results:
- A reduction in the number of calls and complaints from faculty and staff compared to the previous software upgrades
- Commendations from faculty and staff on the process, as well as the ease of use of the manual and the new system
- Personal recognition from the software consultants on a smooth transition

Education
Centreville Community College, Centreville, MO 63633
- Associate's Degree in Computer Servicing Technology (AAS)
- Grade-point average (GPA) 3.75

Achievements ❹
- *Integration of new system software.* Directed campus-wide integration of new computer system software, resulting in an on-time delivery schedule.
- *Lead trainer.* Trained campus faculty and staff in the use of computer systems and software, resulting in a time savings of 6 hours per employee.

❸ Sandra lists a shortened version of her contact information at the top of the second page of her resume. She also includes a "Page 2" designation, which would help in the event that the pages of her resume become unattached.

❹ List any achievements, awards, or other honors after your employment history. Each of these components also should appear in reverse-chronological order.

Hybrid Resume

A **hybrid resume** combines the format of a skills resume with that of a reverse-chronological resume. In a hybrid resume, you first spotlight specific skills, then list your work experience in reverse-chronological order. Hybrid resumes are ideal for those candidates seeking to align developing skills with a rather limited work history. Such candidates include those newer to the workforce, those with gaps in employment, and former military personnel.

❶ In this format, Luis still lists his objective first. His objective should connect to both his background and his employment history.

❷ Luis then lists his qualifications beneath the **Professional Background** section and above his relevant work history. This follows the skills resume format, enabling a hiring manager to focus on Luis' qualifications.

❸ After listing his qualifications, Luis then lists his employment history and education, training, and achievements, using the reverse-chronological resume format.

Luis M. Orazi
515 Hanover St., Atmore, AL 36427
h: 251-555-2991 c: 251-555-2867
l.orazi@pax.com

Objective

To work as an Emergency Medical Technician (EMT) supervisor, bringing my personal and professional skills to a challenging work environment.

Professional Background

- Superior skills as an Emergency Medical Technician, responding to a variety of emergency calls in an urban environment
- Alabama State EMT advanced certification and valid motor vehicle operator's license with excellent driving record
- National Registry of Emergency Medical Technicians certification
- American Red Cross Professional Rescuer
- Physical and mental ability to work in a challenging emergency medical environment, to think critically, and to use independent judgment in routine and non-routine situations
- Excellent communication and interpersonal skills that combine to produce and maintain strong relationships with management, fellow EMTs, and volunteers
- Ability to take direction, follow instructions carefully, and delegate

Related Employment

Emergency Medical Technician, Mobile, AL   June 2009 to Present
- Perform patient assessment and provide advanced triage treatment
- Operate a variety of medical devices and equipment following approved treatment protocols
- Exchange information with nurses and doctors in the Emergency Room as well as between EMTs on incoming and outgoing shifts
- Check medical equipment, vehicles, and tools to ensure working order

Voluntary Firefighter, Rabun, AL   March 2008 to June 2009
- Maintained emergency vehicles such as fire trucks and ambulances
- Delivered public safety education
- Member of search-and-rescue and fire management operations teams

Technical Certifications and Degrees

Lurleen B. Wallace State Jr. College, Andalusia, AL
- EMT—Advanced, 2011
- EMT—Basic, 2009

Leadership Recognition

2011 recipient of the Outstanding Team Member Award for Leadership; Selected for prestigious EMT Accelerated Leadership Development Supervisor Training Program

Curriculum Vitae

A **curriculum vitae**, commonly known as a CV, emphasizes a candidate's academic achievements. A CV offers an excellent format for those with lengthy academic careers but limited job histories. Candidates who use CVs tend to be professors or researchers at colleges and universities. However, some research positions in the business world may prefer or even require the submission of a CV instead of a standard resume.

Jacinda M. Hernandez, Ed.D.
1861 Hyacinth Street, Calabasas, CA 91302
(818) 555-6250
jhernandez@pax.com

❶ Curriculum Vitae

CAREER OBJECTIVE: A skilled and qualified educational leader with years of teaching and leadership experience who seeks to use acquired knowledge and expertise to positively impact a college or university through effective organization, communication, and leadership.

PROFESSIONAL OVERVIEW—EDUCATIONAL LEADERSHIP

More than 20 years of experience in education

- ESL/ELL program coordination
- Direct support of classroom teachers
- Teacher staff development
- One-on-one work with students
- Classroom teaching experience
- ESL paraprofessional experience

❷ EDUCATION AND CREDENTIALS

Ed.D., Educational Leadership, "An Analysis of ELL Program Integration: Examining Shared Traits of Successful Implementations," University of California, Los Angeles, 2006
M.A., Education, Educational Leadership and Administration, University of California, Los Angeles, 2002
B.S., Elementary Education, ELL Certification, University of the Pacific, 1996

❸ PROFESSIONAL EXPERIENCE

Los Angeles Unified School District (LAUSD), Los Angeles, CA

ESL/ELL Program Coordinator (2006 to Present)
  Design, implement, and coordinate ESL/ELL programming for LAUSD
  Assess individual school programs and provided feedback. Organize ESL/ELL teacher training.
  Achievement(s):
  - Improved scores in reading and mathematics for all ESL/ELL learners in LAUSD over a 4-year period.

Itinerant ESL Teacher (2003 to 2006)
  Provided ESL support in elementary classrooms; worked with individual students on reading and writing skills
  Achievement(s):
  - Reduced classroom discipline issues
  - Increased integration of non-English speaking and English-speaking students
  - Improved scores in reading and mathematics

San Luis Obispo School District, San Luis Obispo, CA

Itinerant ESL Teacher (2002 to 2003)
ESL/Reading Resource Teacher (1999 to 2002)
  Provided ELL support in elementary classrooms; worked with individual students on reading and writing skills
  Achievement(s):
  - Improved scores in reading and mathematics
  - Improved reading and writing skills

Page 1 of 3

---

❶ Curriculum vitaes are often longer than one or two pages since they emphasize a complete history rather than a concise snapshot of one's employment and educational past.

❷ Here, Jacinda lists her educational history first, since education is the focus of this format. As such, candidates should list all of their degrees, not just the advanced ones.

❸ As with a standard resume, Jacinda lists her professional experience in reverse-chronological order.

Curriculum Vitae, *page 2*

Although a CV includes some of the same components as a resume, it features some unique differences. For example, a CV includes:

- Description of a dissertation, or a research paper prepared by a candidate pursuing a doctoral degree

- Teaching and research experience
- Publications and presentations
- Areas of specialization or interest
- Honors and awards
- References

Jacinda M. Hernandez, Ed.D. **Page 2**
(818) 555-6250 jhernandez@pax.com

Elementary Teacher (1996 to 1998)
Taught 3rd and 4th grade students in all subjects. Assisted in training of ESL/ELL paraprofessionals.
Achievement(s):
- All students showed progress in all subjects
- Developed training curriculum for ESL/ELL paraprofessionals

ESL Paraprofessional (1988 to 1992)
Assisted classroom teachers with English-language learning students. Instructed small groups of ESL/ELL students. Aided students in understanding and completing of assignments.
Achievement(s):
- Helped students achieve a homework completion rate of 90%.

PRESENTATIONS AND PUBLICATIONS

Forthcoming	"The Current State of English Language Learner Instruction in Southern California." *Trends in ESL/ELL Programming in Elementary Education*. Ed. David Johnson, Enrique Villareal. Provo, UT: Alta.
2009	"Implementing Integrated ELL Services on a Large Scale: Challenges and Accomplishments." <u>TESOL Quarterly</u> 36 (1): 36-40.
2008	"Reforming ELL Instruction in Elementary Classrooms: A District-Wide Approach." <u>42nd TESOL Conference & Exhibit</u>. New York, NY.
2005	"Keeping the Student in the Classroom: Integrated ELL Support." <u>Internet TESL Journal</u>. Vol. XI, No. 3, March 2005. Web.

AREAS OF SPECIALIZATION

ELL Teaching Strategies
ESL Mainstreaming
ESL/ELL Assessment
ELL Program Implementation / Management

AWARDS

2006	*Dean's Scholar Award*, UCLA Graduate School of Education & Information Studies
2004	*Educational Administration Scholarship*, American Association of School Administrators

PROFESSIONAL ASSOCIATIONS

TESOL: Member since 1999
CATESOL: Member since 1998
California Teachers Association: Member 1996 to 2006

CERTIFICATIONS

1998	California Teacher of English Language Learners Certification

SERVICE

2005	Volunteer, 39th TESOL Conference & Exhibit

---

4 On a CV, you will list any academic papers you have written or any presentations you may have made at conferences in your field.

5 Along with **Areas of Specialization**, Jacinda includes awards, professional associations, certifications and service to round out her CV.

Curriculum Vitae, *page 3*

Along with published materials, a CV enables candidates to list papers, manuscripts, or books that are in progress. In addition, candidates may list academic honors, which are key achievements for those who have been out of the mainstream workforce while pursuing advanced degrees.

Those applying for teaching positions or research positions should use a CV, as should those applying for fellowships or entry into academic programs (such as a Ph.D. program). In most cases, an application will specifically state the need for a CV, rather than a resume.

Jacinda M. Hernandez, Ed.D.   **Page 3**
(818) 555-6250   jhernandez@pax.com

6 LANGUAGES

    Spanish (native)
    English

REFERENCES

    Gloria Velasquez
    Professor of Education
    University of California, Los Angeles
    Los Angeles, CA 90095
    310-555-1897

7
    Linda McDonough
    Professor of Education
    University of California, Los Angeles
    Los Angeles, CA 90095
    310-555-1889

    Albert Vanderwal
    Superintendent, Los Angeles Unified School District
    Los Angeles, CA 90017
    805-555-2332

6 Jacinda lists on her CV languages in which she's fluent. If, like Jacinda, you speak multiple languages, you should list them on your resume or CV.

7 Unlike other resume formats, you should include references as part of your CV. If you instead are using a resume, you can include a line at the end of it that states "References available upon request."

Page 3 of 3

Importance of Format

As you've learned, resumes include much of the the same information. However, they often differ in how they present that information.

Below and on the next page you'll see two versions of Alisha Peters' resume—the reverse-chronological format and the skills format.

REVERSE-CHRONOLOGICAL FORMAT

❶ A hiring official first will read a candidate's objective statement, despite the fact that it appears beneath his or her contact information.

❷ Alisha's work experience includes a gap of more than one year. In the eyes of a hiring official that gap may extend even longer since Alisha's position as a day care provider relates only minimally to the job she's now seeking.

❸ However, Alisha's previous position as an administrative assistant relates directly to the job that she's seeking.

ALISHA M. PETERS

1405 33rd Street ◆ Appleton, WI 54911 ◆ 920-555-0047 ◆ Peters.A@pax.com

❶ Objective

To obtain employment as an executive assistant for a major corporation.

Work Experience

In-home Day Care Provider   ❷ February 2006–August 2009
Appleton, WI

> Provided care for up to four other children in my home in addition to my own two children. Coordinated meals, outings, naps, and daily reports to parents.

Administrative Assistant   August 2002–December 2004
Meyer's Insurance, Appleton, WI

> Administrative assistant to a group of four at an insurance company. Answered phones, scheduled appointments and travel, created and polished presentations, handled correspondence, set up meetings and conference calls.

Receptionist   March 1998–July 2000
Sanderson's Hardware, corporate offices, Appleton, WI

> Receptionist for the main phone system at the corporate office. Handled incoming calls, routed them to the correct personnel or departments, managed voicemails. Assisted with mail distribution and other administrative activities as time allowed.

Education

Fox Valley Technical College, Appleton, WI
Administrative Professional Associate's Degree   2002

---

❹ Because her degree as an administrative professional could set her apart from other candidates who are seeking the same position, Alisha may want to rearrange her resume, to better spotlight her education.

As you look at each resume, can you spot differences between the two? What are the advantages of each format? Disadvantages?

Of the two resumes, which format do you think Alisha should use at this point in her career? Which format do you think you should use?

SKILLS FORMAT

ALISHA M. PETERS

1405 33rd Street ◆ Appleton, WI 54911 ◆ 920-555-0047 ◆ Peters.A@pax.com

Objective

To obtain employment as an executive assistant for a major corporation using my past experience as an administrative assistant and my administrative professional degree.

Qualifications

Administrative professional with extensive experience in all aspects of administration of a large, busy office. Currently hold an Associate's Degree as an Administrative Professional. Experienced at multi-tasking in a fast-paced environment. Excellent office management skills.

Administrative Support
- Performed all administrative and secretarial duties for a team of four.
- Scheduled and booked all travel and fulfilled related travel expense reports.
- Scheduled and set up all conference calls and meetings.
- Assisted in the production of presentations.

Reception
- Answered and routed calls for a large corporate office of 200 people.
- Managed the voicemail system, including the establishment of new mailboxes.
- Assisted with other administrative duties, such as incoming and outgoing mail and scheduling of meetings.

Education

Fox Valley Technical College, Pinehurst, NC
- Administrative Professional Associate's Degree – 2002

Employment History
- In-home Day Care Provider, self-employed, Appleton, WI, 2006–2009
- Administrative Assistant, Meyer's Insurance, Appleton, WI, 2002–2004
- Receptionist, Sanderson's Hardware, Corporate Offices, Appleton, WI 1998–2000

❶ In this more thorough objective, Alisha highlights her associate's degree as an administrative professional, an achievement that others seeking this job may lack.

❷ Rather than list her employment history, Alisha begins with a paragraph that summarizes her skills and qualifications, followed by supporting bullets that reinforce her skills and abilities.

❸ In a skills resume, candidates like Alisha often list their educational outcomes before their employment histories.

❹ Alisha's **Employment History** lists only those positions she has held and the length of employment at each. Her expanded skills section makes up for a lack of described duties in **Employment History**.

LESSON REVIEW

▶ Assessment

1. A candidate with both experience and skills should use what type of resume format?
2. Which format would be best for a candidate with extensive academic achievements?
3. Describe the resume format that you're most likely to use for your own resume. Explain why this format represents the best choice for you.

Plain-Text Resume Format

GOALS

EXAMINE the importance and attributes of ASCII plain-text resumes

LEARN how to develop an ASCII plain-text resume

TERMS

PDF

white space

You've already spent considerable time writing and formatting your resume. However, you can develop another version of your resume, known as an ASCII (as ˙ KEE) plain-text resume, in just a few minutes and with only a few keystrokes. ASCII stands for American Standard Code for Information Interchange. An ASCII plain-text resume contains the same information as a formatted resume but lacks much of the formatting common to word-processing documents.

Today, more than 80 percent of employers recruit online via various job boards such as Monster.com or CareerBuilder.com as well as on their own company Web sites. Many of them use applicant-tracking systems (ATS) to record and rank their candidates. Many of these systems accept both formatted and ASCII plain-text resumes. Some, however, *only* accept ASCII resumes, which can be "read" regardless of applicant-tracking system. Resumes formatted in a word-processing application, such as Microsoft Word, sometimes can be viewed only if the hiring manager has the same computer application or system. If not, they can't.

Many hiring officials today prefer to receive resumes via email. If you're attaching a copy of your formatted resume to an email, you also may copy and paste your plain-text resume into the body of the email. Doing so gives a hiring manager the choice of whether to open the attached formatted version based on issues such as system compatibility, virus protection, and the company's policy on opening attachments. You also may convert the resume to a **PDF**, or portable document format, version.

Because some companies and hiring managers today use Adobe Acrobat Reader (a free download) more than they do costly word-processing programs, candidates may be well-suited in sending their resumes to hiring officials as a PDF, rather than as a word-processing document.

Creating an ASCII Plain-Text Resume

If you already have a skills, reverse-chronological, or hybrid resume or a curriculum vitae, you may easily convert it to a plain-text resume. Read below to find out how Anu created an ASCII plain-text resume. Then use the information to help create your own plain-text resume.

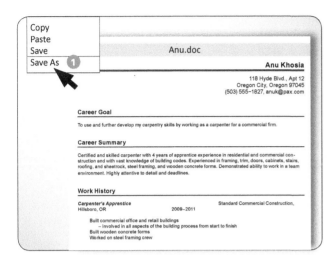

1 Open your formatted resume. Use the "Save As" function of your word-processing program to save a new file of your resume. (You also could copy the text of your resume and paste it into a new file.) Next, change the file name and save it as a plain-text or text-only file by adding a *.txt* extension. Depending on the type and version of your word-processing program, you may need to select "Other Formats" in order to find the *.txt* extension.

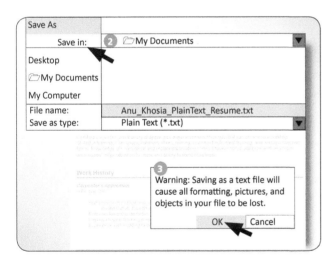

2 Choose the location in which to save your file, such as "My Documents" or your desktop. Include your name in the file name, as Anu did: *Anu_Khosia_PlainText_Resume.txt*.

3 You might receive a warning about losing your formatting. Don't worry. You want to remove the formatting. Click *OK*.

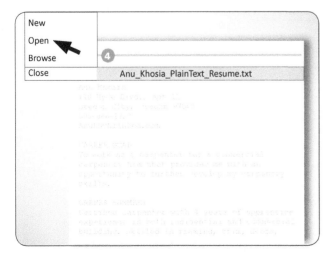

4 Open your word-processing program. (If you open your document without first opening your word processing program, you may see your plain-text resume appear in a program such as Notepad or WordPad. If this happens, simply cut and paste your plain-text resume content into a word-processing document to edit.) Next, select "All Files (*.*)" from the menu called *Files of type*. You then should be able to double-click on your file and view it as a new plain-text resume.

From Formatted to Functional

When you convert your resume from a formatted to a plain-text (*.txt*) version, you lose most or all of the resume's formatting. Most plain-text resumes look similar to the example below and generally share these features:

- A simple, plain-text font, such as Courier 12 point
- Limited formatting through the use of capital letters, asterisks (in place of bullets), and keyboard symbols
- Text justified to the left
- **White space**, or paragraph returns between lines, to break up text
- Line lengths of 80 characters (the total letters, numbers, and spaces per line) or less

With plain-text resumes, what candidates may lose in formatting they then gain in functionality. After all, plain-text resumes allow for easy submission to a series of electronic applicant-tracking systems.

Anu's resume requires further editing before it can be considered final. For example, the blue arrows below indicate additional lines, spaces, and paragraph indents for deletion, while the hollow bullet must be converted to an asterisk (*) and the line of text indented.

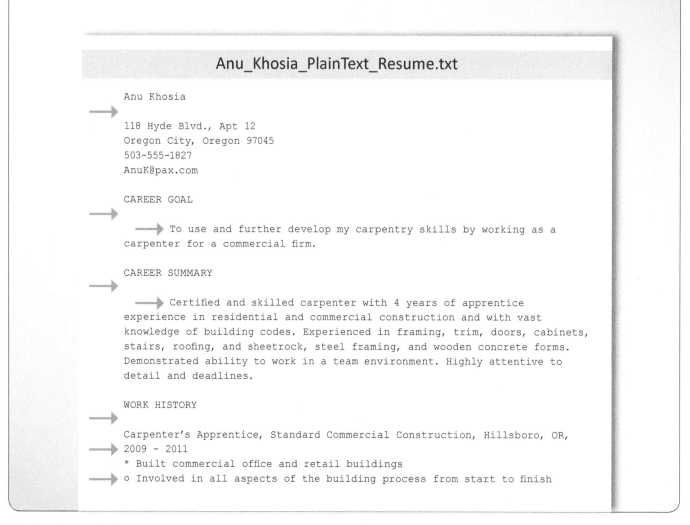

Anu_Khosia_PlainText_Resume.txt

```
Anu Khosia

118 Hyde Blvd., Apt 12
Oregon City, Oregon 97045
503-555-1827
AnuK@pax.com

CAREER GOAL

     To use and further develop my carpentry skills by working as a
carpenter for a commercial firm.

CAREER SUMMARY

     Certified and skilled carpenter with 4 years of apprentice
experience in residential and commercial construction and with vast
knowledge of building codes. Experienced in framing, trim, doors, cabinets,
stairs, roofing, and sheetrock, steel framing, and wooden concrete forms.
Demonstrated ability to work in a team environment. Highly attentive to
detail and deadlines.

WORK HISTORY

Carpenter's Apprentice, Standard Commercial Construction, Hillsboro, OR,
2009 - 2011
* Built commercial office and retail buildings
o Involved in all aspects of the building process from start to finish
```

As you examine Anu's resume both on the previous page and below, you'll note that she made a variety of edits to arrive at a cleaner overall appearance. You can apply the same treatment to your plain-text resume. When finished, save and close the file. Next, print, review, and edit it prior to submission.

PLAIN-TEXT FORMAT

```
Anu Khosia
118 Hyde Blvd., Apt 12
Oregon City, Oregon 97045
503-555-1827
AnuK@pax.com

CAREER GOAL
To use and further develop my carpentry skills by working as a carpenter for a
commercial firm.

CAREER SUMMARY
Certified and skilled carpenter with 4 years of apprentice experience in
residential and commercial construction and with vast knowledge of building
codes. Experienced in framing, trim, doors, cabinets, stairs, roofing, and
sheetrock, steel framing, and wooden concrete forms. Demonstrated ability to
work in a team environment. Highly attentive to detail and deadlines.

WORK HISTORY
Carpenter's Apprentice, Standard Commercial Construction, Hillsboro, OR,
2009 - 2011
* Built commercial office and retail buildings
    Involved in all aspects of the building process from start to finish
* Built wooden concrete forms
* Worked on steel framing crew
* Experience with building codes for commercial buildings

Carpenter's Apprentice, R and L Homebuilders, Inc., Hillsboro, OR,
2007 - 2009
* Worked on various projects from start to finish, including new residential
homes, additions and remodels
    Experienced in framing, trim, doors, cabinet installation, stairs, roofing,
    and sheetrock
* Competent with all hand tools and air tools used in typical carpentry

Warehouse Associate, Building Supply Warehouse, Beaverton, OR,
2006 - 2007
* Operated forklift in loading and unloading lumber inventory
* Operated horizontal band saw, cut-off saw, and banding machine
* Pulled and shipped lumber product orders to stores

TECHNICAL LICENSES AND CERTIFICATIONS
* Carpenter's Certification, Northwest College of Construction, Portland, OR, 2011
* GED credential, Portland Community College, Portland OR, 2006

MEMBERSHIPS
* Member - United Brotherhood of Carpenters and Joiners of America
* Member - Northwest Regional Council of Carpenters
```

1 Align contact information so that it runs together.

2 Use an easy-to-read font such as Courier 12 point.

3 Use only capital letters for headings.

4 All text should be left-justified. The text will wrap automatically.

5 Replace symbols, such as bullets, with asterisks.

6 When possible, leave at least one line of white space between sections. This makes the document easier to read, both for an automated scanner and a hiring manager.

LESSON REVIEW

▶ Assessment

1. Explain the importance of an ASCII plain-text resume.

2. What features do most plain-text resumes have in common?

3. Anu saved her resume in a plain-text format. What should she do next?

4. Use information from the lesson to develop and save a plain-text resume.

Pathways

Joel Brennan uses an architectural design program to create residential and commercial construction plans.

Using the Web to Promote Your Career

You've heard the saying, "A picture is worth a thousand words." An e-Portfolio, or e-folio, provides just that—and then some—as a visual representation of your knowledge, skills, abilities, and core competencies.

An e-folio seldom replaces a resume. Instead, it can provide professionals with an opportunity to showcase their skills and talents in a dynamic, electronic format.

An effective e-folio must:

- market you and your products or ideas
- highlight your skills, talents, and accomplishments
- engage the reader visually
- allow for quick scanning by the reader

As you can see in the table to the right, an e-folio may be created to promote any number of professions, from designers to mechanics.

E-FOLIO EXAMPLES

Graphic Designer

Interior Designer

Event Planner

Chef

Mechanic

Sales Consultant

Editor

Florist

Now, examine Joel's e-folio on the next page. How well does it meet the above criteria?

Potential employers or clients may click the *Sustainable Design* tab to learn more about Joel's commitment to using green construction methods.

Like many creative professionals, Joel constructed an e-folio to showcase examples of his architectural designs.

Chapter Recap

Using the list below, place a checkmark next to the goals you achieved in Chapter 2.

▶ **In Lesson 1, you . . .**

☐ Examined resume components

☐ Learned ways to incorporate each component into your resume

▶ **In Lesson 2, you . . .**

☐ Learned the purpose of various resume formats

☐ Examined the role of a curriculum vitae

☐ Understood the importance of resume formatting

▶ **In Lesson 3, you . . .**

☐ Examined the importance and attributes of ASCII plain-text resumes

☐ Learned how to develop an ASCII plain-text resume

Chapter Review

CHAPTER 2

Name: _____ Date: _____

▶ **Directions:** Match the terms in the left column to the correct definition in the right column.

_____ 1. reverse-chronological
_____ 2. curriculum vitae
_____ 3. hybrid resume
_____ 4. skills resume

A. a type of resume that emphasizes a candidate's employment experience and achievements by listing the most recent position first, followed by the next most recent, and so on

B. a type of resume that emphasizes a candidate's skills and strengths over experience

C. a type of resume that emphasizes a candidate's academic achievements

D. a type of resume that emphasizes both a candidate's skills and employment experience

▶ **Directions:** Choose the best answer.

5. A resume typically includes all of the following elements EXCEPT

   A. contact information.
   B. fancy design treatments.
   C. work experience.
   D. achievements and awards.

6. A candidate with little professional experience should use which of the following resume formats?

   A. reverse-chronological
   B. curriculum vitae
   C. hybrid resume
   D. skills resume

7. Which of the following is true about hiring officials and resumes?

   A. They usually only spend an average of 10 minutes per resume.
   B. They prefer skills resumes over other formats, such as reverse-chronological resumes.
   C. They expect to receive error-free submissions.
   D. They routinely read resumes that exceed 2 pages.

▶ **Directions:** Determine whether the following statements are true or false. If the statement is true, write T. If the statement is false, write F. Then rewrite the false statement to make it true.

8. A candidate's experience level typically determines the components they include in a resume.

_____

_____

_____

9. Plain-text or ASCII resumes allow candidates to easily submit their resumes to applicant-tracking-systems.

_____

_____

_____

▶ **Directions:** Write your answer to the question on the lines below.

10. Describe the process of writing the *Work Experience* section of your resume.

_____

_____

_____

_____

_____

_____

Name: _____ Date: _____

▶ **Directions:** Use the reading and your own experience to complete the resume below.

11.

Career Goal

_____

_____

_____

Qualifications Summary

_____

_____

_____

Work History

_____

_____

_____

_____

_____

Work History (continued)

_____

_____

_____

_____

_____

_____

Education / Training / Certification

_____

_____

_____

Honors/Awards

_____

_____

_____

Cover Letters

▶ **LESSON 1:**

Types of Cover Letters

▶ **LESSON 2:**

Writing a Winning Letter

▶ **LESSON 3:**

Formatting and Editing

▶ **LESSON 4:**

Putting It All Together

Chapter Recap

Chapter Review

☑ ——— ———

☑ ——— ———

☑ ——— ———

▶ **CHAPTER 3**

Recap/Review

Types of Cover Letters

TERMS

cover letter

letter of interest

networking

networking letter

referral letter

internship

internship letter

Resumes often get top billing among job seekers. As for cover letters, well, that's another story entirely. Candidates usually put considerable time and effort into writing and refining their resumes. However, for many candidates cover letters are little more than an afterthought.

That's too bad, since a **cover letter** serves as the entry point for your a job application/resume packet. A cover letter provides candidates with their first, best chance to communicate both their interest and expertise to hiring officials.

As you'll see on the pages that follow, candidates may choose from various types of cover letters, each of which serves a specific purpose:

- Job application cover letter
- Interest/Inquiry cover letter
- Networking cover letter
- Referral cover letter
- Internship cover letter

Cover letters provide candidates with an opportunity to describe both their interest and expertise to hiring officials.

Job Application Cover Letter

As you know, an application and a resume describe your work history and skills. A cover letter, however, provides greater context, or detailed explanation, of your career goals. For example, in the letter below Lucinda applies for a dental hygienist position, a point she also likely makes on her accompanying application or resume. However, the letter enables Lucinda to describe her range of experience in various aspects of dental hygiene. In general, a job application letter like the one below should attempt to persuade a hiring manager to act—whether it means reading your application or resume or calling you for an interview.

---

(1) Lucinda Morez
1634 Mace Drive
Canton, OH 44706
(330) 555-5843
lmorez@pax.com

December 6, 2012

Dr. Stafford
Great River Dental
185 Canyon Way
Canton, OH 44705

Dear Dr. Stafford,

(2) I've been a dental hygienist for 15 years and would love to bring my experience, expertise, and enthusiasm to the open position of Dental Hygienist at your clinic.

I received my degree from Norwood Dental Hygiene School and hold a state license in Ohio. Currently, I'm working as a Dental Hygienist at the Canton Community Clinic. However, I'd like to move to a smaller clinic environment that would allow for enhanced patient interaction.

My extensive experience in dental hygiene care includes:
(3)
- Advising individuals and communities on dental hygiene, with an emphasis on prevention of dental disease
- Performing dental examinations and using them to make diagnoses; consulting with and referring to dentists when necessary
- Cleaning teeth, whitening teeth, and placing fittings
- Performing certain types of prosthetic work and assisting in surgical work
- Working with patients with mental and physical disabilities
- Preparing and maintaining dental equipment

Please consider my credentials and experience, reflected on the enclosed resume, in your search for a Dental Hygienist. I can be reached at the above email and street addresses and phone number. In addition, I'll plan to call you in 10 days to discuss this position. Thank you for your time and consideration.

Sincerely,

Lucinda Morez

Lucinda Morez
(4) Enclosure: Resume

---

(1) Lucinda positions her full contact information—the same information that appears atop her resume—at the top of her cover letter.

(2) Because hiring officials spend very little time reading cover letters, Lucinda immediately states her experience, education, and license status.

(3) Lucinda lists her experience and qualifications in an easy-to-read bulleted format for the hiring manager.

(4) To guard against her application materials becoming separated, Lucinda notes the enclosure of her resume.

Interest/Inquiry Letter

Sometimes a candidate may send a letter to a company even though the company may lack an appropriate opening. This type of letter, known as a **letter of interest**, alerts a company and its hiring manager to your interest in working for them. When writing this type of cover letter—also known as a letter of inquiry or a prospecting letter—you should try to remember the audience. Although *about* you, a cover letter is not *for* you. Instead, the audience for this and other cover letters is a hiring official.

For that reason, you should *think* like a hiring manager. For example, *What would I want to see from an applicant?* Often, that involves connecting your qualifications with a company's needs. In an interest, inquiry, or prospecting letter, you should both explain why the company interests you and also how your skills and experience would benefit the company. By describing and maintaining your interest in this manner, you may gain access to job opportunities—perhaps sooner rather than later—that previously did not exist.

1 Ethan immediately states his connection and personal experience with this company, letting a hiring manager know of his interest—and time frame—in joining the company as an employee.

2 Here, Ethan summarizes his interest, emphasizes his potential value to the company, and outlines a plan for action and for follow-up. This combines to further underscore Ethan's interest in working for First State Bank.

Ethan K. Wallin
437 Shady Oak Terrace
Kansas City, KS 66119
(913) 555-2119
ekwallin@pax.com

September 12, 2012

David Burnet, Human Resources Director
First State Bank
5445 11th Street
Kansas City, KS 66113

Dear Mr. Burnet,

1 As a loyal customer of First State Bank for many years, I've always been impressed with the way the bank conducts business. I am currently finishing my Bachelor's degree in Accounting and will sit for the CPA exam in June 2013, at which time I'll be looking for an accountant position. From my knowledge of your bank, I believe that my accounting and personal skills fit well with First State Bank's business philosophy and would be an asset to you.

Presently, I serve as a university office assistant in the Accounting Department, an annual appointment that goes to a senior who displays exemplary academic and leadership skills. In that capacity, I provide a variety of assistance to first-year accounting students. In addition to excelling at my coursework, I've gained practical experience in the audit department of a small accounting firm. Last summer, I helped an accounts receivable division of an industrial machinery company update their accounting software and systems.

2 I've enclosed my resume for your consideration, and would love the opportunity to discuss with you in person my background, qualifications, and work ethic that together can make a significant contribution to First State Bank. I will telephone you in the next week to answer any questions or needs you may have of me. Thank you for your time and consideration.

Best Regards,

Ethan Wallin

Ethan Wallin
Enclosure: Resume

Networking Letter

When most people hear the term *networking*, they think of computers. When searching for a job, though, the term **networking** refers to the exchange of information or services among individuals, groups, or institutions. When you network, you create productive relationships for employment or to expand your business. Networking can be a valuable tool in the job market. Through friends, coworkers, family members, or at events, you may meet people who become part of your network.

The purpose of a **networking letter** involves asking for career advice and assistance. A networking cover letter includes letters of introduction, referral letters, letters requesting a meeting, and letters asking for career advice. You may send this kind of letter—either by email or traditional mail—to a friend or former colleague, someone you recently met, or a person to whom you were referred. Web sites such as LinkedIn provide another means by which to network with fellow professionals.

Ajay Sarin
6840 Long Leaf Drive
Bakersfield, CA 93307
(661) 555-0851
ASarin@pax.com

May 23, 2012

Dr. Lydia Connor
President, Innovative Plastic Design
185 Canyon Way
Bakersfield, CA 93301

Dear Dr. Connor:

1 You may recall that we met last week at the Chemical Engineering Conference in San Francisco, during which time I very much enjoyed learning about your company. I'm writing to ask whether we might be able to continue the conversation, in particular to discuss the types of projects on which you're currently working.

2 For the past six years, I've worked as a chemical engineer with a focus on metal processing. However, I'm now highly interested in making a move to plastics engineering. To that end, I'm hopeful for any advice or guidance you may have about career opportunities in, or transitions to, this field. I've enclosed my resume for your review as a possible discussion point.

As a next step, I'll plan to contact you next week to hopefully arrange a brief meeting at your convenience. If you would prefer to contact me, I may be reached at the phone number and email address listed above.

Sincerely,

Ajay Sarin

Ajay Sarin

1 When using a networking cover letter, recall the place, date, and/or time of an initial meeting in the first sentence.

2 Using a networking letter to ask for advice can be a great way by which to gain a meeting—and information—regardless of whether it occurs by phone or in person.

Referral Letter

You may hear from someone in your network about an opportunity at a company. If so, you may decide to send a **referral letter** to that company, in which you mention in the opening paragraph the name of the person who referred you.

By doing so, you may immediately grab the attention of a hiring official. Because applicant-tracking systems today automate much of the hiring process, a referral from a person connected with a company can carry weight with HR officials.

❶ Here, Keith Long mentions the source of the referral, Eric Rodriguez, in the opening paragraph of his letter. This lets the hiring official, Dan Montgomery, know that Eric can speak to Keith's qualifications for the job.

❷ Keith provides a brief overview of his skills, qualifications, and experience that support the referral.

❸ By using the words "like you," Keith provides insight into values he shares with the company, Ivy Industries.

Keith Long
525 Eighth Street
North Pekin, IL 61554
309-555-1847
Long.K@pax.com

August 8, 2012

Dan Montgomery
Ivy Industries
58 Ivy Way
Bartonville, IL 61607

Dear Mr. Montgomery:

❶ My friend, Eric Rodriguez, suggested that I contact you regarding your job opening for a first-shift machinist. He enjoys working for Ivy Industries and speaks highly of the work environment. Based on our conversations, he believes that I might be a good fit for the position.

❷ I've worked as a machinist for more than 10 years, including my current position at Metalworks, Ltd., a range of experience that would benefit Ivy Industries. As a professional, I'm committed to working both carefully yet efficiently. In particular, I enjoy helping co-workers resolve issues that improve workflow and results. In addition, I've had the opportunity to work on various machines and learn about new ones.

❸ I'm quite knowledgeable about Ivy's products and, like you, believe in the company's ideals of providing a good product at a fair price. To that end, I'd like an opportunity to explore the position further with you, perhaps in an interview setting. I'll plan to call you next week to follow up and discuss next steps in your search for a first-shift machinist.

Best Regards,

Keith Long

Keith Long

Enclosure: Resume

Internship Letter

Some college and certification programs require students to complete an **internship**, or a paid or unpaid position at a company in which they have interest. An internship provides both experience and connections that they may use in their career.

In an **internship letter**, you should explain to an employer your qualifications for an internship. Because an internship usually lasts for only a few months, such as over a summer, you should inform the company when you'll be available to start.

Maya Denton
316 Beckman Ave, #4
Montana, MT 59802
(406) 555-5603
mayad@pax.com

January 14, 2012

Lucy Love
Montana State Parks Summer Internship
1045 East Fifth Avenue
Helena, MT 59620

Dear Ms. Love:

① I am writing to express my interest in becoming a summer intern for Montana State Parks. I am an avid outdoorswoman and believe my previous experience as a nature center guide, along with my educational background in ecology, would serve the Montana State Parks well as a summer intern. I am particularly interested in the interpretive guide internship.

Currently, I'm a junior at the University of Montana double-majoring in ecology and biology. My specific interests are in endangered species and habitat protection. Upon graduation, I hope to begin a career with the U.S. Fish and Wildlife Service.

In addition to my coursework in biology and ecology, I worked last summer as a nature guide. In that capacity, I led tours and taught various classes for first and second graders. Enclosed please find a resume for your review.

② I very much look forward to the opportunity to work within the Montana State Parks system. I am available May 8 through September 10. I look forward to speaking with you further and answering any questions you may have.

Sincerely,

Maya Denton

Maya Denton

Enclosure: Resume

---

① Internships can be very competitive! For that reason, immediately state your interest, relevant experience, and/or educational background that together support your candidacy for the position.

② Maya understands the importance of planning ahead by writing her letter January 14, nearly four months before the end of school and the start of the internship. That leaves Maya ample time to interview by phone or in person for the internship.

LESSON REVIEW

▶ Assessment

1. Why should a candidate include a cover letter with an application or a resume?

2. Compare and contrast the goals of an inquiry letter with the goals of a networking letter.

3. Why should you mention a referral source in the opening paragraph of a referral letter?

4. List companies to which you plan to send cover letters, and describe the type(s) of letters that you'd send to them.

Writing a Winning Letter

GOALS

LEARN the standard components of a cover letter.......85–95

EXAMINE in detail the components of a cover letter ..86–95

APPLY your knowledge by writing part of your cover letter 95

TERMS

opening salutation

closing salutation

As you know, a cover letter tells your story. It describes your interests, education, work history, and career goals—all in a single narrative. It provides context for your career history and offers insight into your achievements. Today, it has become a must-have part of the application process. Two-thirds of hiring managers in a national survey said that they prefer that a candidate includes a strong cover letter with a resume. In another survey, a similar percentage of executives believe the cover letter to be *more important* than the resume.

In many ways, a job search is like an obstacle course. You must clear previous hurdles before you can move on to new ones. To that end, your cover letter becomes the opening act for your resume. If done properly, the cover letter encourages a hiring official to read your resume. "The cover letter is the elevator pitch for your resume," notes the president of a Massachusetts-based consulting firm. "It's your best bet for grabbing the recruiter's interest so that the recruiter wants to review your resume."

A well-written cover letter can help describe your career goals and experience and encourage a hiring official to then read your resume.

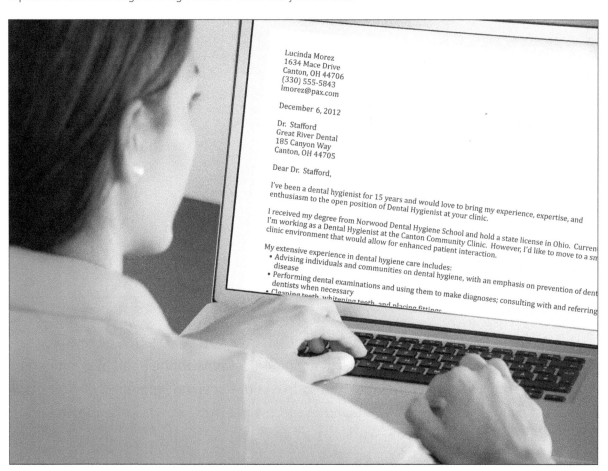

Cover Letter Components

Cover letters run about three to five paragraphs in length and include these components: an **opening salutation**, or greeting; an opening paragraph; middle paragraphs; a closing paragraph; and a **closing salutation**, or end.

1

LINDSAY WAITE
2140 Ivey Lane, Orlando, FL 32789
Home: 407-555-9711
Cell: 407-555-7245
lwaite@pax.com

2 May 1, 2012

2 Ms. Karen Lloyd
Director, Human Resources
Center City Children's Hospital
13535 Children's Parkway
Orlando, FL 32789

3 Dear Ms. Lloyd,

4 It was with great excitement that I recently read your job advertisement for a patient relations representative for the Center City Children's Hospital. As a recent graduate of the University of Central Florida with a bachelor's degree in Health Services Administration, I'm not sure I could have a found a more perfect opportunity.

5 I love working with people and have great compassion for children and families in need of medical assistance. Most recently, I interned with the American Diabetes Association. In that role, I was chosen to advocate for the *Tour de Cure* fundraiser. That assignment involved scheduling, coordinating, and receiving donations from many local businesses, all of which enabled me to leverage my organizational and interpersonal skills. In addition, I also coordinated all event communications, including keeping all key fundraising members current with the progress of the event. Throughout this fundraiser, I met and worked with many wonderful children and families. As a result, I've concluded that my true passion lies in working with children and families. As a Center City team member, I pledge to give the children and families in my charge the utmost in attention and service.

6 I'd very much like the opportunity to meet with you to further discuss this position and learn more about the possibility of becoming a member of a top-flight patient care team at Center City Children's Hospital. I am available at your convenience to meet with you, and may be reached at the phone number and email address listed above and on my enclosed resume. Thank you in advance for your consideration, and l will follow up next week to schedule an appointment. I look forward to speaking with you soon.

7 Sincerely,

Lindsay Waite

Lindsay Waite
8 Enclosure: Resume

1 Your contact information always should appear at the top of your letter. You should include your street address (including city, state, and zip code), home and cell phone numbers, and email address.

2 Add the date of the letter two paragraph returns below your contact information and two paragraph returns above the hiring manager's contact information. The contact information for the hiring manager should include his or her name, title, company, and address.

3 Your opening salutation should be placed two paragraph returns below the hiring manager's contact information.

4 In your opening paragraph, you should state your purpose for writing (e.g., the position for which you're applying). If applicable, mention the name of any referral source.

5 Your middle paragraph(s) represent the meat of your letter. They should describe your experience, qualifications, achievements, and goals.

8 List any attachments or enclosures that accompany your letter. These may include resumes, transcripts, or even work samples.

7 Your closing salutation should be two paragraph returns beneath the end of the closing paragraph.

6 In your closing paragraph, try to refer the reader to the accompanying resume (or application form), reiterate your interest, and list relevant next steps.

Opening Salutation

When you're writing a cover letter or preparing to send an email message to apply for a job, you should include an appropriate opening salutation at the beginning of your cover letter or message. In the salutation, you should attempt to include the name of the hiring official. At times, this may involve some detective work on your end. You may use any of a host of networking sites, such as LinkedIn, or even call the company to learn the name of the relevant hiring official.

In general, even an educated guess trumps a generic salutation such as "To Whom It May Concern." However, double-check both the spelling of the person's name and his or her title, especially if receiving that information over the phone. Most mistakes in a cover letter are simple misspellings of names and addresses. Often, employers discard application materials for even a simple error. You then can conclude the salutation with a colon or comma before beginning the opening paragraph of your letter.

SALUTATIONS

Strong Opening Salutations

Dear Mr. Smith
Dear Ms. Smith
Dear Jane Doe
Dear Dr. Jones

Weak Opening Salutations

Dear Hiring Manager
To Whom It May Concern
Dear Sir or Madam
Dear Human Resources Manager
Greetings

CLIVE • SERVICE

❶ Dear Ms. Jennings:

❶ The job posting to which Clive plans to respond specifies that resumes be sent to the attention of the hiring manager, Evelyn Jennings.

ANU • SKILLED TRADE

❷ Dear Mr. Luger:

❷ Although the job posting failed to list the name of the hiring manager, Anu called the company and learned it was Mr. Luger.

❸ Dear Mr. Schlafke,

I am writing about the Field Technician/Help Desk Technician job vacancy posted on the Employment page of your company's Web site. I have experience working in desktop and network systems support

❸ Sandra addresses her opening salutation to "Mr. Schlafke," exactly how it was written in the job advertisement. Sandra prefaces his name with the word "Dear," a common opening to letters.

❹ Dear Ms. Grossman,

Jada Rathmore, a former coworker and current EMT with Mobile EMS, suggested that I apply for your open position of Emergency Medical Technician supervisor. I've been an EMT since 2009 and completed

❹ The job advertisement specified responses be sent to the attention of Katherine Grossman. Since Luis doesn't know Katherine Grossman's marital status, he uses the less specific "Ms." to address her in the cover letter.

❺ Dear Dr. Hamilton,

I am writing on the recommendation of Dr. Ribak, Professor of Curriculum and Instruction at Paxon State University. I recently discussed my upcoming relocation to the Paxon area with Dr. Ribak and it was during our conversation

❺ If you're sending a cover letter to a professional with credentials, such as Dr. Hamilton, ensure that you include their title (Dr.) prior to their name. It shows respect for their position.

Opening Paragraph

The opening paragraph sets the tone for the rest of your cover letter. It describes your interests and outlines your goals. In many respects, it will be the most important part of your cover letter. Hiring managers only spend a matter of seconds reviewing application materials, so candidates like you must get—and keep—their attention.

In particular, this section of your letter should clearly explain your reasons for writing (e.g., your interest in a specific position) and ways in which your skills and abilities align with the opening. Avoid generic sentences such as, "I am applying for the customer service position listed in the newspaper" in favor of more targeted ones like, "Your opening for a customer service professional represents an ideal match with my experience as a successful call center manager."

If a friend or family member referred you to this position, mention their name in the opening paragraph. That connection alone may encourage a hiring manager to continue reading your letter and, hopefully, to advance to your resume.

CLIVE • SERVICE

1 I was delighted to learn from your online posting of an opening for a front-desk clerk at The Queen's Inn. I'm currently pursuing a degree in hotel management and believe that my excellent customer service skills and educational background combine to make me an ideal fit for this position.

1 In the opening paragraph of his cover letter seeking a front-desk position, Clive effectively blends his customer-service experience with his continuing education in hotel management.

ANU • SKILLED TRADE

2 Whether it's helping construct rooms or entire buildings, I love carpentry. Recently, I saw a flyer at Northwood College of Construction advertising your need for a carpenter. I am a talented carpenter whose experience and skill in residential and commercial building would be an asset to JL and Company Construction. I enjoy a challenging, fast-paced environment and look forward to adding my skills to the JL and Company team.

2 Anu immediately explains her passion for carpentry, followed by her interest in the position at JL and Company Construction. Anu also mentions the value that she would bring to the company as a carpenter.

③ I am writing about the Field Technician/Help Desk Technician job vacancy posted on the Employment page of your company's Web site. I have experience working in desktop and network systems support and recently completed my Associate's Degree in Computer Servicing Technology at Centreville Community College. My experience and background will enable me to hit the ground running in a new position.

③ Sandra explains that the combination of her experience and education in information technology will allow her to quickly transition and contribute to the organization as a Field Technician/Help Desk Technician.

④ Jada Rathmore, a former coworker and current EMT with Mobile EMS, suggested that I apply for your open position of Emergency Medical Technician supervisor. I've been an EMT since 2009 and completed my Advanced EMT training in 2011. I'm seeking a supervisory role that combines my strengths in field experience and interpersonal communication while providing additional challenges and responsibility.

④ Luis explains his desire to advance to a supervisory EMT position by noting his education, experience, and willingness to embrace new challenges and responsibility.

⑤ I am writing on the recommendation of Dr. Ribak, Professor of Curriculum and Instruction at Paxen State University. I recently discussed my upcoming relocation to the Tuscon area with Dr. Ribak and it was during our discussion that he mentioned an opening for an Assistant TESOL Professor in the College of Education. Dr. Ribak believes that I'd make an excellent candidate to fill this opening. I received my Ed.D. in Educational Leadership from the University of California, Los Angeles, in 2006, and am currently the ESL/ELL Program Coordinator for the Los Angeles Unified School District.

⑤ Jacinda details her referral, Dr. Ribak, as well as her desire to relocate to the Tuscon area. She also clearly explains her educational and teaching backgrounds, both of which are highly relevant to the TESOL opening.

Middle Paragraph(s)

If your opening paragraph acts as an appetizer—getting the attention of a hiring manager—then the middle paragraph or paragraphs are the main course. They *keep* a hiring official's attention through the use of specific examples that connect your skills and abilities to the position for which you're applying.

Depending on your level of experience, the middle section may be only a single paragraph or it may be as long as two or three paragraphs. In general, you should write only as much as you need to tell your story, since hiring managers usually have little time in which to review materials. Use that space wisely to describe in detail your education and experience, noteworthy achievements, and career goals. It always helps to thoroughly research a company and include in your cover letter news or statistics that relate to the position for which you're applying.

❶ In my position at Hayes Department Store, I've had the opportunity to work closely with customers. In particular, I take great satisfaction in *their* satisfaction as customers. To that end, I've streamlined the process by which returns and exchanges are handled, making it much faster and easier for customers. This streamlining also has increased the number of returned items that may be placed immediately back on the sales floor.

❶ Clive provides an example of his commitment to customers through his streamlining of the store's return policy. In so doing, he shows how his skills might transfer to a front-desk position.

❷ In 2011, I completed my Carpenter's Certification from the Northwood College of Construction. As a carpenter's apprentice, I worked both with a homebuilder and a commercial construction company. As an apprentice with the homebuilder, I was fortunate to work on nearly every aspect of homebuilding, including framing, trim, doors, cabinets, stairs, roofing and sheet rock. In commercial building, my experience emphasized wooden concrete forms and steel framing. I am very focused, disciplined, and motivated to bring my carpentry talents to JL and Company Construction.

❷ Anu describes her duties and responsibilities, including the experience and skills she acquired as an apprentice in home construction.

3 I am excited about the prospect of bringing skills that I've gained as a desktop support specialist and network systems technician to support Jancom's mission of improving operational efficiencies and enhancing client service levels. I'm very interested in the opportunity to work both with a Field Support team, as well as independently in setting up temporary job sites and providing desktop support. I believe that my previous experience in desktop support and setting up and maintaining networks at a large and varied organization has prepared me for the challenges in managing the setup, installation, and maintenance required by your clients. As stated in my attached resume, I've had experience across multiple operating platforms and in setting up and maintaining network systems.

3 Sandra aligns her skills and experience with Jancom's goals of operational efficiencies, while providing detail about her experience, including across multiple platforms.

4 Due to the smaller nature of LifeCare Ambulance Services, I've had an opportunity to gain experience in responding to emergency situations and in working in every aspect of the emergency medical response team. My passion, however, lies in working with people and sharing my knowledge with them. Such skills and experiences make me an ideal candidate for the position of EMT supervisor, and will help ensure the continuous, smooth operation of your ambulance service.

4 Luis connects his skills and experience to LifeCare's need for smooth ambulance operations.

5 I have experience at every level of ESL/ELL programming, from classroom teacher to district-wide program coordinator. I began my career as an elementary school teacher and pursued my interest in ESL/ELL first as a resource teacher and then later as an ESL/ELL specialist. My work in the schools influenced my research interests in developing more efficient ESL/ELL programs.

My dissertation and research focus both on current best practices in ESL/ELL education and more specifically on effective implementation of these methodologies and successful integration with mainstream educational curriculum. The combination of my academic and professional experiences has uniquely prepared me for both research and teaching. My extensive knowledge of current practices in elementary education guides my research interests and helps me to prepare students who are studying to work in the field. I've spent the majority of my career connected in some way to the classroom. Whether working on reading skills with elementary school children or training colleagues in teaching methodologies, I've always enjoyed the challenges and rewards of classroom teaching. As ESL/ELL Program Coordinator, I've enjoyed the exchange of ideas with colleagues as well as leading and participating on organizational committees.

5 Jacinda's body paragraphs offer significant details into her breadth and depth of experience in ESL/ELL education.

Closing Paragraph

Use the closing paragraph of your cover letter as an opportunity to summarize your main points and reiterate your interest in and enthusiasm for the position. In particular, provide a phone number(s) or email address at which the hiring official may contact you. This contact information should match that at the top of your cover letter. You also should outline targeted next steps. Since hiring officials often are quite busy, you may mention that you'll reach out to them to discuss the opening. If so, ensure that you provide a day and a time that you'll be calling—and stick to it. If applying from outside the employer's geographic area, you may want to indicate a date that you'll be in town and available to interview.

CLIVE • SERVICE

① In closing, I believe my customer service, office, and technical skills will be a great asset to the team in general and the front-desk position in particular at The Queen's Inn. I am attaching my resume for your review and will plan to call next Wednesday to answer any questions you may have. Thank you for your time and consideration.

① Clive summarizes his experience, connects it to employer needs, and outlines next steps in his closing paragraph.

ANU • SKILLED TRADE

② I am ready to take the next step in my career and look forward to the opportunity to speak with you in depth about the carpenter position. I am available for an interview at your convenience, either in person or by telephone at the number above. Thank you for your time, and I'll plan to follow up by phone on Friday, March 16, at 10 a.m.

② In her closing, Anu reiterates her interest in working at a higher level as a carpenter. She also provides a date and a time by which to follow up with the position.

SANDRA • INFORMATION TECHNOLOGY

3 I welcome the opportunity to meet with you to further discuss this position and learn more about this exciting opportunity to become a member of a first-class IT support provider such as Jancom. I am available at any time to meet with you, either by phone or videoconference or in person. You may reach me at the phone number and email address listed above and on my resume. In closing, I appreciate your time and consideration, and look forward to speaking with you soon.

3 Along with the possibility of talking on the phone or in person, Sandra extends the possibility of meeting via videoconference, which helps support her IT experience.

LUIS • HEALTHCARE

4 I'm highly excited and intrigued by your opening for an EMT supervisor, and would love to discuss it with you at your earliest possible convenience. Enclosed please find a copy of my resume. Next week, I'll plan to call your office to schedule a convenient time to discuss the position and to answer any questions you may have. Thank you in advance for your consideration, and I can't wait to discuss the position with you next week.

4 Luis' closing paragraph contains words such as "highly excited," "intrigued," and "can't wait" that reveal his enthusiasm for the EMT supervisory position.

JACINDA • EDUCATION

5 I look forward to sharing both my teaching and professional experience with the students and faculty at Paxen State University. To that end, enclosed please find copies of my CV, transcripts, and contact information for my professional references. I would be more than happy to provide any other documentation upon request. I am available at the contact information listed above. Thank you for your consideration.

5 In contrast to Luis' closing paragraph and its enthusiasm, Jacinda's closing paragraph uses a more formal style better suited to a position in higher education.

Closing Salutation

Your cover letter should include a closing salutation. The most common salutations are "Sincerely," "Respectfully," "Regards," "Kind regards," and "Best regards." If possible, avoid syrupy salutations such as "Yours Truly." If you plan to print and sign the letter, as opposed to emailing it, insert four lines of space between the salutation and your name. Place your signature in this area.

You should sign your letter using the same name that appears on your resume (e.g., "Sandra" rather than "Sandy"). Beneath your signature, you may include the term "Enclosure." This refers to another part of your application that you're submitting with your cover letter. If you're submitting both a resume *and* an application, you would write at the bottom of your cover letter "Enclosures: resume and application."

❶ Regards,

Clive Robinson

Clive Robinson

Attachment: Resume

❶ Clive uses the word "Regards," which blends formal with casual and caring.

❷ Sincerely,

Anu Khosia

Anu Khosia

❷ Anu uses perhaps the most common salutation, "Sincerely," to close her letter.

❸ Kind Regards,

Sandra L. Brown

Sandra L. Brown

Attachment: Resume

❸ One of the best all-around salutations, "Kind Regards" suggests warmth to the reader.

❹ With anticipation,

Luis Orazi

Luis Orazi

Enclosure: Resume

❹ Luis' use of "With anticipation" supports his overall excitement about the opportunity.

❺ Respectfully,

Jacinda Hernandez

Jacinda Hernandez, Ed.D.

Enclosures: Curriculum Vitae, Transcripts, Professional References

❺ Jacinda's closing of "Respectfully" aligns with the rest of her letter. She also notes the enclosures that accompany her application.

LESSON REVIEW

▶ Assessment

1. What are the standard components of a cover letter?
2. In what ways can opening and closing salutations affect your cover letter?
3. Why would a candidate include only one middle paragraph in a cover letter?
4. Why should a candidate mention that he or she plans to contact the hiring official?
5. Write a sentence for an opening paragraph of your cover letter. In the opening paragraph, explain your purpose for writing the letter.

CHAPTER 3

LESSON 3

Formatting and Editing

GOALS

LEARN to properly format a cover letter

. 96–97

EXAMINE strategies for editing your cover letter 98–109

UNDERSTAND the importance of a professional, error-free cover letter

. 108–109

Hiring officials have tough jobs. At any one time, they may be trying to fill many different openings across a variety of locations. They likely use an applicant-tracking system to help score and rank candidates' applications. Then, they quickly scan the top-rated cover letters and resumes for those that appear most promising. On average, hiring officials spend less than 1 minute—and sometimes less than 30 seconds—reviewing one resume. That means applicants must quickly convey their qualifications. You should seek to make their jobs easier by properly formatting and editing your cover letter. Examine below and on the next page Luis' cover letter, formatted first for a hard-copy submission and then for electronic delivery.

1 Luis uses tabs within his word-processing application to right-justify his contact information, an accepted look with hard-copy or print submissions.

2 Luis uses simple formatting throughout the document. He chooses to use an easy-to-read font, Arial, and avoids use of any graphics, such as pictures. Hiring officials usually discard applications if they include photographs of candidates. That way, companies reduce their risk of racial or gender discrimination lawsuits from applicants.

3 A hard-copy submission enables Luis to include an enclosure, such as a resume, with his cover letter.

---

1   **Luis M. Orazi**
515 Hanover St.
Atmore, AL 36427
cell: 251-555-2867
l.orazi@pax.com

November 14, 2012

Katherine Grossman
Mobile EMS
163 Mississippi Drive
Mobile, AL 36607

Dear Ms. Grossman,

2 Jada Rathmore, a former coworker and current EMT with Mobile EMS, suggested that I apply for your open position of Emergency Medical Technician supervisor. I've been an EMT since 2009 and completed my Advanced EMT training in 2011. I'm seeking a supervisory role that combines my strengths in field experience and interpersonal communication while providing additional challenges and responsibility.

Due to the smaller nature of LifeCare Ambulance Services, I've had an opportunity to gain experience in responding to emergency situations and in working in every aspect of the emergency medical response team. My passion, however, lies in working with people and sharing my knowledge with them. Such skills and experiences make me an ideal candidate for this position, and will help ensure the continuous, smooth operations of your ambulance service.

I'm highly excited and intrigued by your opening for an EMT supervisor, and would love to discuss it with you at your earliest possible convenience. Enclosed please find a copy of my resume. Next week, I'll plan to call your office to schedule a convenient time to discuss the position and to answer any questions you may have. Thank you in advance for your consideration, and I can't wait to discuss the position with you next week.

With anticipation,

Luis Orazi

3 Enclosure: Resume

Plain-Text Cover Letter

In today's world of lean human resources staffs and applicant-tracking systems, most applications, resumes, and letters are delivered electronically. In Chapter 2, we discussed the need to prepare a plain-text, unformatted resume for online submissions. The same need applies for your cover letter. As with your ASCII or electronic resume, you'll want to format your cover letter so that it may be read by an applicant-tracking system. To that end, you'll use capital letters, asterisks, and keyboard symbols as your main formatting options. Leave white space between lines to break up text and justify it to the left. Use an easy-to-read font such as Courier *(see letter, below)* for electronic submissions.

Along with preparing a formatted resume for mailed or in-person submissions, Luis wants to develop a plain-text letter that he may use for electronic applications. In preparation, he reviewed the steps outlined in Chapter 2, Lesson 3, for converting formatted documents to plain text and saving them as a text-only, or *.txt*, application.

Luis knows he must treat a plain-text cover letter the same way he would a formatted version. That means printing, editing, and finalizing an error-free letter before submitting it. Luis' completed plain-text cover letter appears below. Compare it against the formatted version that appears on the facing page. What similarities or differences do you see?

```
① November 14, 2012

Katherine Grossman
Mobile EMS
163 Mississippi Drive
Mobile, AL  36607

Dear Ms. Grossman,

Jada Rathmore, a former coworker and current EMT with Mo-
bile EMS, suggested that I apply for your open position of
Emergency Medical Technician supervisor. I've been an EMT
since 2009 and completed my Advanced EMT training in 2011.
I'm seeking a supervisory role that combines my strengths
in field experience and interpersonal communication while
providing additional challenges and responsibility.

Due to the smaller nature of LifeCare Ambulance Services,
I've had an opportunity to gain experience in responding
to emergency situations and in working in every aspect of
the emergency medical response team. My passion, however,
lies in working with people and sharing my knowledge with
them. Such skills and experiences make me an ideal candi-
date for this position, and will help ensure the continu-
ous, smooth operations of your ambulance service.

I'm highly excited and intrigued by your opening for an
EMT supervisor, and would love to discuss it with you at
your earliest possible convenience. Enclosed please find a
copy of my resume. Next week, I'll plan to call your office
to schedule a convenient time to discuss the position and
to answer any questions you may have. Thank you in advance
for your consideration, and I can't wait to discuss the
position with you next week.

With anticipation,

Luis Orazi
515 Hanover St.
Atmore, AL 36427
cell: 251-555-2867
l.orazi@pax.com
②
```

① Luis began his letter with the date and the recipient's contact information. He opted to place his contact information beneath, with the signature line falling at the bottom of the letter.

② Unlike the hard-copy cover letter, Luis doesn't list an enclosure on his plain-text letter. Instead, he'll likely submit his resume in a separate part of the online application.

Editing Your Cover Letter

Just as Luis did, you'll want to review and refine your cover letter prior to submitting it. After all, your cover letter likely will be the first communication that a hiring official will have from you. You want to make it count. Although a strong cover letter will not guarantee you a job, a poorly written one can eliminate you from consideration. Indeed, a well-written cover letter should encourage a hiring official to read your resume and hopefully then contact you for an interview.

As we've noted, hiring officials have limited time in which to review cover letters and resumes. If they find misspellings, incorrect information, and/or poor writing or grammar skills, your candidacy may be over before it ever begins.

Instead, you should seek to help hiring officials—and yourself—by preparing a professional cover letter that catches and keeps their attention. Since you only have a few seconds of a hiring official's time, you should seek to produce a perfect cover letter that avoids:

- *Misspellings and simple typographic errors.* These errors can creep into a document, sometimes in unlikely places such as an envelope or email subject line. Hiring officials have little tolerance for these errors. For that reason, you should plan to review all materials at least twice before submission.

- *A lack of customization.* Often, candidates may apply to multiple openings in a single day. In such instances, they must update their cover letter, including the name of the company, the contact, and the position, for each submission. As a general guide, you should develop a master cover letter document. You then should do a "save as" and rename the file for each opportunity you're pursuing.

STRONG VS. WEAK COVER LETTERS

Category	Strong Letters . . .	Weak Letters . . .
Address	Include the name of a specific hiring official	Use vague salutations ("Dear Sir or Madam")
Emphasis	Detail what you can do for a potential employer	Detail what a potential employer can do for you
Purpose	Highlight and extend information in your resume	Repeat information from your resume
Length	Run less than one page	Exceed one or two pages
Editing	Include proper grammar, punctuation, and spelling	Feature poor grammar, punctuation, and spelling
Formatting	Feature clear, easy-to-read formatting	Include poor, hard-to-read formatting

STEPS FOR EDITING YOUR COVER LETTER

The following process shows steps for editing your cover letter.

1 Use your computer's spell-check function to help catch spelling mistakes.

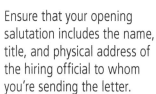

2 Ensure that your opening salutation includes the name, title, and physical address of the hiring official to whom you're sending the letter.

3 Next, check the name, title, and physical address of the person to whom you're sending the letter for errors. Often, you may use professional networking sites such as LinkedIn to check information about hiring officials.

4 Check details in your letter, such as the title of the position for which you're applying.

5 Run another spell-check on your cover letter. Then print and review it to check for and eliminate any remaining errors in spelling, grammar, punctuation, and accuracy.

Unedited Cover Letter 1

Once you've written your cover letter, take a break before you edit it. When you're ready to edit it, you should review your application materials at least twice before submitting them. You also may want a third party, such as a friend or family member, to review your cover letter for you.

On the pages that follow, you'll see unedited and edited cover letters from Clive, Anu, Sandra, Luis, and Jacinda. The unedited cover letters will highlight the most common errors on cover letters. Then, note changes our job seekers make to ensure professional, error-free cover letters.

1 The date should appear below your contact information but above the hiring manager's contact information.

2 Your letter should grab the reader's attention. Here, Clive's opening sentence lacks detail (there may be multiple clerk vacancies) and misspells the company's name.

3 This sentence repeats the beginning part of the second sentence in the first paragraph. It shows a hiring official that Clive failed to proofread his cover letter before submission.

---

1 September 17, 2012

CLIVE T. ROBINSON
7254 Ashland Ave.
Raeford, NC 28376
910-555-7504
Clive.Robinson@pax.com

Evelyn Jennings
Hotel Manager
The Queen's Inn
750 Everett Street
Fayetteville, NC 28305

Dear Ms. Jennings,

2 I just saw your advertisement for a clerk at Queens In. I'm currently pursuing a degree in hotel management and believe that my excellent customer service skills and educational background combine to make me an ideal fit for this position.

In my position at Hayes Department Store, I've had the opportunity to work closely with customers. In particular, I take great satisfaction in *their* satisfaction as customers. To that end, I've streamlined the process by which returns and exchanges are handled, making it much faster and easier for customers. This streamlining also has increased the number of returned items that may be placed immediately back on the sales floor. **3** I'm currently pursuing a degree in hotel management.

In closing, I believe my customer service, office, and technical skills will be a great asset to the team in general and the front-desk position in particular at The Queen's Inn. I am attaching my resume for your review and will plan to call next Wednesday to answer any questions you may have. Thank you for your time and consideration.

Regards,

Clive Robinson

Edited Cover Letter 1

As you can see below, Clive made some strong changes to his cover letter. For starters, he rewrote the first sentence of his opening paragraph to include greater detail and accuracy. Clive's letter also now displays a certain enthusiasm for the position through his use of the word "delighted."

Additionally, Clive moved the date to the proper place and reformatted his contact information so that it better stands out. He also proofread the letter to remove any redundancy, or repetition. Through his edits, Clive produced a professional, error-free cover letter.

1 **Clive T. Robinson**
7254 Ashland Ave ◆ Raeford, NC 28376
910-555-7504 ◆ Clive.Robinson@pax.com

2 September 17, 2012

Evelyn Jennings
Hotel Manager
The Queen's Inn
750 Everett Street
Fayetteville, NC 28305

Dear Ms. Jennings,

3 I was delighted to learn from your online posting of an opening for a front-desk clerk at The Queen's Inn. I'm currently pursuing a degree in hotel management and believe that my excellent customer service skills and educational background combine to make me an ideal fit for this position.

In my position at Hayes Department Store, I've had the opportunity to work closely with customers. In particular, I take great satisfaction in *their* satisfaction as customers. To that end, I've streamlined the process by which returns and exchanges are handled, making it much faster and easier for customers. This streamlining also has increased the number of returned items that may be placed immediately back on the sales floor.

In closing, I believe my customer service, office, and technical skills will be a great asset to the team in general and the front-desk position in particular at The Queen's Inn. I am attaching my resume for your review and will plan to call next Wednesday to answer any questions you may have. Thank you for your time and consideration.

Regards,

Clive Robinson

4 Attachment: Resume

1 By placing his contact information in the center of the document, Clive draws more attention to it.

2 Clive moved the date between his contact information and that of the hiring manager.

3 Clive rewrote his opening sentence to reflect greater detail, accuracy, and enthusiasm. When editing your cover letter, put yourself in the hiring manager's shoes. Does your opening sentence and paragraph make you want to keep reading?

4 When enclosing or adding an attachment, ensure that you note it beneath your name. This will alert a hiring manager to be on the lookout for your documents.

Unedited Cover Letter 2

Just like a billboard promotes a product, your cover letter and resume help sell you to companies and hiring officials. As your chief marketing tools, your cover letter and resume list your career goals, achievements, and qualities and qualifications that you'd bring to an organization.

A well-written cover letter whets the appetite of a hiring manager. It generates enthusiasm for your candidacy and hopefully drives a hiring official to take action by emailing or calling you for an interview. In short, if you take care of your cover letter, it will help take care of you, too.

① Avoid using a weak opening salutation.

② Check carefully for misspelled words. Some words may be spelled correctly, but have a different meaning. Here, Anu should use the word *flyer*, which means an informational document, rather than *flier*, or someone who flies.

③ The presence of silly errors, such as a missing period or the word "the," can suggest sloppiness to an employer.

Anu Khosia
118 Hyde Blvd, Apt 12
Oregon City, OR 97045
503-555-1827
AnuK@pax.com

March 10, 2012

JL and Company Construction, LLC
58 Ivy Way
Bartonville, IL, 61607

① To Whom it May Concern:

② Whether it's helping construct rooms or entire buildings, I love carpentry. Recently, I saw a flier at Northwood College of Construction advertising your need for a carpenter. I am a talented carpenter whose experience and skill in residential and commercial building would be an asset to JL and Company Construction. I enjoy a challenging, fast-paced environment and look forward to adding my skills to the JL and Company team.

③ In 2011, I completed my Carpenter's Certification from the Northwood College of Construction As a carpenter's apprentice, I worked both with a homebuilder and a commercial construction company. As an apprentice with the homebuilder, I was fortunate to work on nearly every aspect of homebuilding, including framing, trim, doors, cabinets, stairs, roofing and sheet rock. In commercial building, my experience emphasized wooden concrete forms and steel framing. I am very focused, disciplined, and motivated to bring my carpentry talents to JL and Company Construction.

③ I am ready to take the next step in my career and look forward to the opportunity to speak with you in depth about the carpenter position. I am available for an interview at your convenience, either in person or by telephone at number above. Thank you for your time, and I'll plan to follow up by phone on Friday, March 16, at 10 a.m.

Sincerely,

Anu Khosia

Edited Cover Letter 2

Anu's edited cover letter shows very few changes from the unedited version. However, the changes she made will help her candidacy. Anu's letter initially included both spelling and punctuation errors, which could damage—or even end—her candidacy.

Anu also used a weak opening salutation in her original letter. However, she later researched and learned the name of the hiring manager. That enabled her to change the salutation from "To Whom It May Concern" to "Dear Mr. Luger" for better relevance.

Anu Khosia
118 Hyde Blvd, Apt 12
Oregon City, OR 97045
503-555-1827
AnuK@pax.com

March 10, 2012

Mr. Donald Luger
Hiring Manager
JL and Company Construction, LLC
58 Ivy Way
Bartonville, IL, 61607

Dear Mr. Luger:

Whether it's helping construct rooms or entire buildings, I love carpentry. Recently, I saw a flyer at Northwood College of Construction advertising your need for a carpenter. I am a talented carpenter whose experience and skill in residential and commercial building would be an asset to JL and Company Construction. I enjoy a challenging, fast-paced environment and look forward to adding my skills to the JL and Company team.

In 2011, I completed my Carpenter's Certification from the Northwood College of Construction. As a carpenter's apprentice, I worked both with a homebuilder and a commercial construction company. As an apprentice with the homebuilder, I was fortunate to work on nearly every aspect of homebuilding, including framing, trim, doors, cabinets, stairs, roofing and sheet rock. In commercial building, my experience emphasized wooden concrete forms and steel framing. I am very focused, disciplined, and motivated to bring my carpentry talents to JL and Company Construction.

I am ready to take the next step in my career and look forward to the opportunity to speak with you in depth about the carpenter position. I am available for an interview at your convenience, either in person or by telephone at the number above. Thank you for your time, and I'll plan to follow up by phone on Friday, March 16, at 10 a.m.

Sincerely,

Anu Khosia

1 Anu called the company and asked for and received the hiring manager's name, Mr. Luger. As a result, her new version reads more professionally than does her previous salutation.

2 Anu corrected the misspelled word *flier to flyer.*

3 Anu added a period after the word "Construction" for correct punctuation.

4 By printing and reviewing her cover letter, Anu saw the omission of the word "the," which enabled her to add it to the final document.

Unedited Cover Letter 3

After you finish writing your cover letter, you'll want to thoroughly edit it. In fact, you'll likely wish to review and edit it at least twice. As you edit the letter, recall the components that make a good cover letter. For example, do your paragraphs flow well in the order in which you've written them?

Would it make more sense to rearrange your ideas? If so, you may use your computer's word-processing program to move words, sentences, and even entire paragraphs within the document. For instance, on its own a sentence may appear to be well written, but in the overall letter it may seem out of place.

❶ Ensure that you include the date on your cover letter.

❷ This sentence requires the use of an apostrophe between the *m* and the *s* for correct grammar and punctuation.

❸ The highlighted sentence lacks details that support Sandra's background and experience.

❹ The letter lacks a closing salutation. Without one, the letter ends in a more formal tone and without an opportunity for the goodwill that a salutation offers.

Sandra L Brown
6702 Sheridan Avenue
St. Louis, MO 63104
(314) 555-9104
slbrown34@pax.com

❶

Mr. Robert Schlafke
Field Support Manager
Jancom IT Support Solutions
821 St. Charles Place
Shrewsbury, MO 63119

Dear Mr. Schlafke,

I am writing about the Field Technician/Help Desk Technician job vacancy posted on the Employment page of your company's Web site. I have experience working in desktop and network systems support and recently completed my Associate's Degree in Computer Servicing Technology at Centreville Community College. My experience and background will enable me to hit the ground running in a new position.

❷ **❸** I am excited about the prospect of bringing skills that I've gained as a desktop support specialist and network systems technician to support Jancoms mission of improving operational efficiencies and enhancing client service levels. I'm very interested in the opportunity to work both with a Field Support team, as well as independently in setting up temporary job sites and providing desktop support. I believe that my previous experience in desktop support and setting up and maintaining networks at a large and varied organization has prepared me for this job.

I welcome the opportunity to meet with you to further discuss this position and learn more about this exciting opportunity to become a member of a first-class IT support provider such as Jancom. I am available at any time to meet with you, either by phone or videoconference or in person. You may reach me at the phone number and email address listed above and on my resume. In closing, I appreciate your time and consideration, and look forward to speaking with you soon.

❹

Sandra L. Brown

Edited Cover Letter 3

In other cases, you may decide in your edit to add detail to further support a point or a claim. If so, ensure that you also review and edit all new material so that you avoid introducing errors. At minimum, you should run a spell check on all new content and then print and review it a second time.

As you can see below, Sandra made a handful of changes to her cover letter, all of which improved the end product. In particular, note that she added information at the end of the second paragraph to provide greater detail about her experience in information technology.

Sandra L Brown
6702 Sheridan Avenue
St. Louis, MO 63104
(314) 555-9104
slbrown34@pax.com

① June 11, 2011

Mr. Robert Schlafke
Field Support Manager
Jancom IT Support Solutions
821 St. Charles Place
Shrewsbury, MO 63119

Dear Mr. Schlafke,

I am writing about the Field Technician/Help Desk Technician job vacancy posted on the Employment page of your company's Web site. I have experience working in desktop and network systems support and recently completed my Associate's Degree in Computer Servicing Technology at Centreville Community College. My experience and background will enable me to hit the ground running in a new position.

② **③** I am excited about the prospect of bringing skills that I've gained as a desktop support specialist and network systems technician to support Jancom's mission of improving operational efficiencies and enhancing client service levels. I'm very interested in the opportunity to work both with a Field Support team, as well as independently in setting up temporary job sites and providing desktop support. I believe that my previous experience in desktop support and setting up and maintaining networks at a large and varied organization has prepared me for the challenges in managing the setup, installation, and maintenance required by your clients. As stated in my attached resume, I've had experience across multiple operating platforms and in setting up and maintaining network systems.

I welcome the opportunity to meet with you to further discuss this position and learn more about this exciting opportunity to become a member of a first-class IT support provider such as Jancom. I am available at any time to meet with you, either by phone or videoconference or in person. You may reach me at the phone number and email address listed above and on my resume. In closing, I appreciate your time and consideration, and look forward to speaking with you soon.

④ Kind Regards,

Sandra L. Brown
Attachment: Resume

① Sandra added the date in the correct location.

② An apostrophe prior to the *s* in *Jancom's* reflects proper grammar and punctuation.

③ Sandra added details to support her experience across multiple platforms and systems.

④ Sandra included the popular closing salutation *Kind Regards* and noted the inclusion of an attachment, her resume.

Unedited Cover Letter 4

As you continue editing your cover letter, you'll note that some errors are more obvious than others. For example, simple typographic errors may be caught by a spell-check program. Others, such as missing or extra words or inaccurate information, require a second, deeper review.

For that reason, a cover letter checklist, such as the one in Appendix D at the back of this book, can be helpful. It will provide you with a series of benchmarks against which to check your cover letter. After you've checked all the boxes, you've completed the edit of your cover letter.

1 Luis' letter lists an incorrect hiring manager (Mr. Williams, rather than Katherine Grossman). This type of error, while common, occurs when cutting-and-pasting sections for customization purposes. A simple spell check will not catch the error.

2 This sentence is a run-on. When a sentence includes a clause, it must be separated by a comma.

3 Luis omitted the word "supervisor" that should follow *EMT*, which could lead to confusion with a hiring official.

Luis M. Orazi
515 Hanover St.
Atmore, AL 36427
cell: 251-555-2867
l.orazi@pax.com

November 14, 2012

Katherine Grossman
Mobile EMS
163 Mississippi Drive
Mobile, AL, 36607

1 Dear Mr. Williams,

Due to the smaller nature of LifeCare Ambulance Services, I've had an opportunity to gain experience in responding to emergency situations and in working in every aspect of the emergency medical response team. My passion, however, lies in working with people and sharing my knowledge with them. Such skills and experiences make me an ideal candidate for the position of EMT supervisor, and will help ensure the continuous, smooth operation of your ambulance service.

2 Jada Rathmore a former coworker and current EMT with Mobile EMS suggested I apply for the position of Emergency Medical Technician supervisor you currently have open. I've been an EMT since 2009 and completed my Advanced EMT training in 2011. I'm seeking a supervisory role that combines my strengths in field experience and interpersonal communication while providing additional challenges and responsibility.

3 I'm highly excited and intrigued by your opening for an EMT, and would love to discuss it with you at your earliest possible convenience. Enclosed please find a copy of my resume. Next week, I'll plan to call your office to schedule a convenient time to discuss the position and to answer any questions you may have. Thank you in advance for your consideration, and I can't wait to discuss the position with you next week.

With anticipation,

Luis Orazi

Enclosure: Resume

Edited Cover Letter 4

Even so, you still may wish to read your letter out loud. Doing so will enable you to decide whether the sentences flow well together. You may find sentences that sound unfinished. In addition, you may wish to have a friend or family member also read your cover letter.

As you can see below, Luis keeps a copy of his cover letter on his computer and customizes it (doing a "save as") for each new opportunity. In so doing, he carefully updates all aspects of his letter to eliminate errors and maximize the letter's effect with hiring officials.

Luis M. Orazi
515 Hanover St.
Atmore, AL 36427
cell: 251-555-2867
l.orazi@pax.com

November 14, 2012

Katherine Grossman
Mobile EMS
163 Mississippi Drive
Mobile, AL, 36607

(1) Dear Ms. Grossman,

(2) Jada Rathmore, a former coworker and current EMT with Mobile EMS, suggested that I apply for your open position of Emergency Medical Technician supervisor. I've been an EMT since 2009 and completed my Advanced EMT training in 2011. I'm seeking a supervisory role that combines my strengths in field experience and interpersonal communication while providing additional challenges and responsibility.

Due to the smaller nature of LifeCare Ambulance Services, I've had an opportunity to gain experience in responding to emergency situations and in working in every aspect of the emergency medical response team. My passion, however, lies in working with people and sharing my knowledge with them. Such skills and experiences make me an ideal candidate for the position of EMT supervisor, and will help ensure the continuous, smooth operation of your ambulance service.

(3) I'm highly excited and intrigued by your opening for an EMT supervisor, and would love to discuss it with you at your earliest possible convenience. Enclosed please find a copy of my resume. Next week, I'll plan to call your office to schedule a convenient time to discuss the position and to answer any questions you may have. Thank you in advance for your consideration, and I can't wait to discuss the position with you next week.

With anticipation,

Luis Orazi

Enclosure: Resume

(1) Luis corrected the name of the hiring official in the salutation. He also removed the phrase "you currently have open" from the firsrt letter in favor of "your open position," which reads better.

(2) Here, Luis used correct punctuation. In addition, because he used a referral to contact Ms. Grossman, Luis moved this paragraph to the top of the letter to grab Ms. Grossman's attention.

(3) Luis included the word "supervisor" in his closing paragraph, which avoids any confusion about the position for which he's applying.

Unedited Cover Letter 5

As you know, the content of your cover letter can encourage a hiring official to continue reading other application materials, such as a resume. However, its appearance can be equally as important. You want to use an easy-to-read font that hiring officials can quickly scan.

In Jacinda's cover letter, she initially opted to use a font that, although the same point size as that on the facing page, appears smaller and more difficult to read. In addition, Jacinda's font choice seems inappropriate to the position—an assistant professor—for which she's applying.

① This font looks juvenile and seems inappropriate for the level of job for which Jacinda's applying.

② Jacinda neglected to include two critical pieces of information, her phone number and email address.

③ Jacinda misspelled Dr. Hamilton's last name, a no-no that could eliminate Jacinda from consideration.

④ Because *pursed* is a word, spell check failed to flag it for correction, even though the word should be *pursued*. To guard against such occurrences, ask a friend or family member to proofread your cover letter.

⑤ The word "have" should be "has" to be grammatically correct.

⑥ Oops! Jacinda forgot to replace the University of New Mexico with Paxen State University. Ensure when proofreading that you fully customize your cover letter to each job for which you're applying.

---

① Jacinda Hernandez
1861 Hyacinth Street
Calabasas, CA 91302

②

February 6, 2012

Dr. Shirley Hamilton, Chair
College of Education
Paxen State University
Tuscon, AZ 85721

③ Dear Dr. Hamelton,

I am writing on the recommendation of Dr. Ribak, Professor of Curriculum and Instruction at Paxen State University. I recently discussed my upcoming relocation to the Tuscon area with Dr. Ribak and it was during our discussion that he mentioned an opening for an Assistant TESOL Professor in the College of Education. Dr. Ribak believes that I'd make an excellent candidate to fill this opening. I received my Ed.D. in Educational Leadership from the University of California, Los Angeles, in 2006, and am currently the ESL/ELL Program Coordinator for the Los Angeles Unified School District.

④ I have experience at every level of ESL/ELL programming, from classroom teacher to district-wide program coordinator. I started my career as an elementary school teacher and pursed my interest in ESL/ELL first as a resource teacher and later as an ESL/ELL specialist. My work in the schools influenced my research interests in developing more efficient ESL/ELL programs.

My dissertation and research focus both on current best practices in ESL/ELL education, and more specifically on effective implementation of these methodologies and successful integration with mainstream educational curriculum. The combination of my academic and professional **⑤** experiences have uniquely prepared me for both research and teaching. My extensive knowledge of current practices in elementary education guides my research interests and helps me to prepare students who are studying to work in the field. I've spent the majority of my career connected in some way to the classroom. Whether working on reading skills with elementary school children or training colleagues in teaching methodologies, I've always enjoyed the challenges and rewards of classroom teaching. As ESL/ELL Program Coordinator, I've enjoyed the exchange of ideas with colleagues as well as leading and participating on organizational committees.

⑥ I look forward to sharing both my teaching and professional experience with the students and faculty at The University of New Mexico. To that end, enclosed please find copies of my CV, transcripts, and contact information for my professional references. I would be more than happy to provide any other documentation upon request. I am available at the contact information listed above. Thank you for your consideration.

Respectfully,

Jacinda Hernandez, Ed.D.
Enclosures: Curriculum Vitae, transcripts, Professional References

Edited Cover Letter 5

In general, you should avoid using fancy fonts and complex designs when developing your cover letter and resume. Instead, you want to keep the focus on your content by choosing one easy-to-read font such as Arial, Calibri, Times New Roman, or Verdana and using it throughout the document.

Note below the positive change that occurred when Jacinda changed her letter's font. The text still fits on page, but it appears more readable. If you encounter issues in fitting your letter onto one page, you can resolve them by simply adjusting the font, point size, and margins.

① Jacinda Hernandez
1861 Hyacinth Street
Calabasas, CA 91302
② 818-555-6250
jhernandez@pax.com

February 6, 2012

Dr. Shirley Hamilton, Chair
College of Education
Paxen State University
Tuscon, AZ 85721

③ Dear Dr. Hamilton,

I am writing on the recommendation of Dr. Ribak, Professor of Curriculum and Instruction at Paxen State University. I recently discussed my upcoming relocation to the Tuscon area with Dr. Ribak and it was during our discussion that he mentioned an opening for an Assistant TESOL Professor in the College of Education. Dr. Ribak believes that I'd make an excellent candidate to fill this opening. I received my Ed.D. in Educational Leadership from the University of California, Los Angeles, in 2006, and am currently the ESL/ELL Program Coordinator for the Los Angeles Unified School District.

④ I have experience at every level of ESL/ELL programming, from classroom teacher to district-wide program coordinator. I began my career as an elementary school teacher and pursued my interest in ESL/ELL first as a resource teacher and then later as an ESL/ELL specialist. My work in the schools influenced my research interests in developing more efficient ESL/ELL programs.

⑤ My dissertation and research focus both on current best practices in ESL/ELL education and more specifically on effective implementation of these methodologies and successful integration with mainstream educational curriculum. The combination of my academic and professional experiences has uniquely prepared me for both research and teaching. My extensive knowledge of current practices in elementary education guides my research interests and helps me to prepare students who are studying to work in the field. I've spent the majority of my career connected in some way to the classroom. Whether working on reading skills with elementary school children or training colleagues in teaching methodologies, I've always enjoyed the challenges and rewards of classroom teaching. As ESL/ELL Program Coordinator, I've enjoyed the exchange of ideas with colleagues as well as leading and participating on organizational committees.

⑥ I look forward to sharing both my teaching and professional experience with the students and faculty at Paxen State University. To that end, enclosed please find copies of my CV, transcripts, and contact information for my professional references. I would be more than happy to provide any other documentation upon request. I am available at the contact information listed above. Thank you for your consideration.

Respectfully,

Jacinda Hernandez, Ed.D.
Enclosures: Curriculum Vitae, Transcripts, Professional References

① Jacinda's new font choice improves the readability of her letter without using any additional space.

② Jacinda added her phone number and email address to the letter.

③ Jacinda corrected the spelling of Dr. Hamilton's name.

④ Jacinda changed the word *pursed to pursued.*

⑤ Jacinda changed the word *have to has.*

⑥ Jacinda added the correct name of the school to which she's applying, Paxen State University.

LESSON REVIEW

▶ Assessment

1. Why should you avoid using fancy fonts, intricate designs, or photos in your cover letter?

2. How does a formatted cover letter differ from a plain-text cover letter?

3. List and explain strategies for editing your cover letter.

4. Why should you strive for a professional, error-free cover letter?

Putting It All Together

Now that you've completed your resume and cover
letter, you need to make sure that they work together. That
means ensuring your content aligns across documents. In particular,
your cover letter should support your resume, and vice-versa.

Clive T. Robinson
7254 Ashland Ave ◆ Raeford, NC 28376
910-555-7504 ◆ Clive.Robinson@pax.com

September 17, 2012

Evelyn Jennings
Hotel Manager
The Queen's Inn
750 Everett Street
Fayetteville, NC 28305

Dear Ms. Jennings,

I was delighted to learn from your online posting of an opening for a front-desk clerk at The Queen's Inn. I'm currently pursuing a degree in hotel management and believe that my excellent customer service skills and educational background combine to make me an ideal fit for this position.

In my position at Hayes Department Store, I've had the opportunity to work closely with customers. In particular, I take great satisfaction in *their* satisfaction as customers. To that end, I've streamlined the process by which returns and exchanges are handled, making it much faster and easier for customers. This streamlining also has increased the number of returned items that may be placed immediately back on the sales floor.

In closing, I believe my customer service, office, and technical skills will be a great asset to the team in general and the front-desk position in particular at The Queen's Inn. I am attaching my resume for your review and will plan to call next Wednesday to answer any questions you may have. Thank you for your time and consideration.

Regards,

Clive Robinson

Clive Robinson

Attachment: Resume

Clive's Cover Letter and Resume

As you can see on the previous page and below, Clive's letter and skills resume spotlight his strengths in customer service and office and technical skills. It also enables Clive to downplay his lack of experience. Instead, he emphasizes his education and transferable skills in customer service. Here and on the pages that follow, you'll see completed cover letters and resumes for Clive, Anu, Sandra, Luis, and Jacinda. As you review their documents, note ways in which they support one another. In addition, examine elements and components in their materials that you may adapt to fit your own style and situation.

Clive T. Robinson

7254 Ashland Avenue ◆ Raeford, NC 28376 ◆ 555-543-7504 ◆ Clive.Robinson@pax.net

---

Customer Service/Hospitality Specialist
**Customer Service • POS System Specialist • Office Management
Telephone Reception • Computer Systems**

INTEREST

To leverage my superior customer-service skills and begin a career in hotel management as a front-desk clerk.

STRENGTHS

Customer Service
- Possess strong communication skills that result in unsurpassed customer service
- Persevere to resolve challenging issues
- Return customer calls promptly and courteously
- Manage customers, provide reassurance, and resolve conflict

Office and Technical
- Understand POS cash register systems, hardware, and software
- Direct the opening and closing of cash registers
- Operate various pieces of office equipment
- Answer and direct customer calls on multi-line phone systems

EDUCATION

**Sandhills Community College,
Pinehurst, NC**
- 15 hours of coursework toward a degree in business management
- High School diploma, Fayetteville (N.C.) High School

EMPLOYMENT EXPERIENCE

Customer Service Representative,   3/2008 to Present
Hayes Department Store, Fayetteville, NC

Customer service position receiving and routing calls to appropriate departments, handling returns and exchanges, assisting with cash register training and troubleshooting, and ensuring customer satisfaction.

AWARDS

Employee of the Year,   2010-2011
Hayes Department Store

Anu's Cover Letter and Resume

Anu's cover letter and resume emphasize her combination of hands-on carpentry skills and educational training. In her closing paragraph, Anu exhibits an eagerness to continue growing her career. Anu remains mindful of her audience in her choice of an easy-to-read font, Arial, for both her cover letter and resume. She also selects the reverse-chronological resume format, which employers prefer, to illustrate her work experience.

Anu Khosia
118 Hyde Blvd, Apt 12
Oregon City, OR 97045
503-555-1827
AnuK@pax.com

March 10, 2012

Mr. Donald Luger
Hiring Manager
JL and Company Construction, LLC
58 Ivy Way
Bartonville, IL, 61607

Dear Mr. Luger:

Whether it's helping construct rooms or entire buildings, I love carpentry. Recently, I saw a flyer at Northwood College of Construction advertising your need for a carpenter. I am a talented carpenter whose experience and skill in residential and commercial building would be an asset to JL and Company Construction. I enjoy a challenging, fast-paced environment and look forward to adding my skills to the JL and Company team.

In 2011, I completed my Carpenter's Certification from the Northwood College of Construction. As a carpenter's apprentice, I worked both with a homebuilder and a commercial construction company. As an apprentice with the homebuilder, I was fortunate to work on nearly every aspect of homebuilding, including framing, trim, doors, cabinets, stairs, roofing and sheet rock. In commercial building, my experience emphasized wooden concrete forms and steel framing. I am very focused, disciplined, and motivated to bring my carpentry talents to JL and Company Construction.

I am ready to take the next step in my career and look forward to the opportunity to speak with you in depth about the carpenter position. I am available for an interview at your convenience, either in person or by telephone at the number above. Thank you for your time, and I'll plan to follow up by phone on Friday, March 16, at 10 a.m.

Sincerely,

Anu Khosia

Anu Khosia

Anu Khosia
118 Hyde Blvd., Apt 12
Oregon City, Oregon 97045
(503) 555-1827, AnuK@pax.com

Career Goal

To use and further develop my carpentry skills by working as a carpenter for a commercial firm.

Career Summary

Certified and skilled carpenter with 4 years of apprentice experience in residential and commercial construction and with vast knowledge of building codes. Experienced in framing, trim, doors, cabinets, stairs, roofing, and sheetrock, steel framing, and wooden concrete forms. Demonstrated ability to work in a team environment. Highly attentive to detail and deadlines.

Work History

Carpenter's Apprentice   Standard Commercial Construction, Hillsboro, OR
2009–2011
- Built commercial office and retail buildings
    - Involved in all aspects of the building process from start to finish
- Built wooden concrete forms
- Worked on steel framing crew
- Experience with building codes for commercial buildings

Carpenter's Apprentice   R and L Homebuilders, Inc., Hillsboro, OR
2007–2009
- Worked on various projects from start to finish, including new residential homes, additions, and remodels
    - Experienced in framing, trim, doors, cabinet installation, stairs, roofing, and sheetrock
- Competent with all hand tools and air tools used in typical carpentry

Warehouse Associate   Building Supply Warehouse, Beaverton, OR
2006–2007
- Operated forklift in loading and unloading lumber inventory
- Operated horizontal band saw, cut-off saw, and banding machine
- Pulled and shipped lumber product orders to stores

Technical Licenses and Certifications

- Carpenter's Certification, Northwest College of Construction, Portland, OR   2011
- GED credential, Portland Community College, Portland OR   2006

Memberships

- Member – United Brotherhood of Carpenters and Joiners of America
- Member – Northwest Regional Council of Carpenters

Sandra's Cover Letter and Resume

Sandra's cover letter reflects and supports her job target and overview statements. In her cover letter, she notes her experience in desktop support through "maintaining networks at a large and varied organization" and her flexibility in working "across multiple operating platforms." Sandra also organizes her resume in a very simple but effective *Challenge / Action / Results* format that describes at a glance her key assignments and outcomes.

Sandra L Brown
6702 Sheridan Avenue
St. Louis, MO 63104
(314) 555-9104
slbrown34@pax.com

June 11, 2011

Mr. Robert Schlafke
Field Support Manager
Jancom IT Support Solutions
821 St. Charles Place
Shrewsbury, MO 63119

Dear Mr. Schlafke,

I am writing about the Field Technician/Help Desk Technician job vacancy posted on the Employment page of your company's Web site. I have experience working in desktop and network systems support and recently completed my Associate's Degree in Computer Servicing Technology at Centreville Community College. My experience and background will enable me to hit the ground running in a new position.

I am excited about the prospect of bringing skills that I've gained as a desktop support specialist and network systems technician to support Jancom's mission of improving operational efficiencies and enhancing client service levels. I'm very interested in the opportunity to work both with a Field Support team, as well as independently in setting up temporary job sites and providing desktop support. I believe that my previous experience in desktop support and setting up and maintaining networks at a large and varied organization has prepared me for the challenges in managing the setup, installation, and maintenance required by your clients. As stated in my attached resume, I've had experience across multiple operating platforms and in setting up and maintaining network systems.

I welcome the opportunity to meet with you to further discuss this position and learn more about this exciting opportunity to become a member of a first-class IT support provider such as Jancom. I am available at any time to meet with you, either by phone or videoconference or in person. You may reach me at the phone number and email address listed above and on my resume. In closing, I appreciate your time and consideration, and look forward to speaking with you soon.

Kind Regards,

Sandra L. Brown

Sandra L. Brown
Attachment: Resume

Page 1 of 2
To view the entire resume, see Chapter 2 Lesson 2

SANDRA L. BROWN 6702 Sheridan Ave., St. Louis, MO 63104 ♦ (314) 555-9104 ♦ slbrown@pax.com

Job Target	To work as an internal technical support team member, bringing my skills in database management and system administration software, as well as installation, maintenance, and repair of desktop and network hardware, to a new and challenging position.
Overview	Network Systems Technician/IT Specialist with 4+ years of experience with network administration and maintenance, system backups, databases, hardware and software for Windows, Macintosh, and Linux operating systems.

Relevant Experience

Network Systems Technician I	Centreville Community College
August 2010 – May 2011	Centreville, MO

Challenge: To ensure a smooth transition for faculty and staff to new software on all campus computers

Action: Interviewed faculty and staff to assess their level of knowledge of the new systems. Based on this information, prioritized the information to be conveyed to staff before, during, and after the transition. Provided faculty and staff with several weeks' notice and a specific timeline of the transition. Wrote and distributed a handbook that simplified use of the new system, including troubleshooting tips.

Results:
- A reduction in the number of calls and complaints from faculty and staff compared to the previous software upgrades
- Commendations from faculty and staff on the process, as well as the ease of use of the manual and the new system
- Personal recognition from the software consultants on a smooth transition

Luis' Cover Letter and Resume

Luis begins his cover letter with a referral, arguably the best strategy for opening doors at companies. He offers context about his role at LifeCare, including his experience working in "every aspect of the emergency medical response team." He next outlines his passion: to work with a team of people—a mission supported by his objective. Luis ends his letter with an enthusiastic closing statement designed to prompt a hiring official to read his resume.

Luis M. Orazi
515 Hanover St.
Atmore, AL 36427
cell: 251-555-2867
l.orazi@pax.com

November 14, 2012

Katherine Grossman
Mobile EMS
163 Mississippi Drive
Mobile, AL 36607

Dear Ms. Grossman,

Jada Rathmore, a former coworker and current EMT with Mobile EMS, suggested that I apply for your open position of Emergency Medical Technician supervisor. I've been an EMT since 2009 and completed my Advanced EMT training in 2011. I'm seeking a supervisory role that combines my strengths in field experience and interpersonal communication while providing additional challenges and responsibility.

Due to the smaller nature of LifeCare Ambulance Services, I've had an opportunity to gain experience in responding to emergency situations and in working in every aspect of the emergency medical response team. My passion, however, lies in working with people and sharing my knowledge with them. Such skills and experiences make me an ideal candidate for the position of EMT supervisor, and will help ensure the continuous, smooth operation of your ambulance service.

I'm highly excited and intrigued by your opening for an EMT supervisor, and would love to discuss it with you at your earliest possible convenience. Enclosed please find a copy of my resume. Next week, I'll plan to call your office to schedule a convenient time to discuss the position and to answer any questions you may have. Thank you in advance for your consideration, and I can't wait to discuss the position with you next week.

With anticipation,

Luis Orazi

Luis Orazi

Enclosure: Resume

Luis M. Orazi
515 Hanover St., Atmore, AL 36427
h: 251-555-2991 c: 251-555-2867
l.orazi@pax.com

Objective

To work as an Emergency Medical Technician (EMT) supervisor, bringing my personal and professional skills to a challenging work environment.

Professional Background

- Superior skills as an Emergency Medical Technician, responding to a variety of emergency calls in an urban environment
- Alabama State EMT advanced certification and valid motor vehicle operator's license with excellent driving record
- National Registry of Emergency Medical Technicians certification
- American Red Cross Professional Rescuer
- Physical and mental ability to work in a challenging emergency medical environment, to think critically, and to use independent judgment in routine and non-routine situations
- Excellent communication and interpersonal skills that combine to produce and maintain strong relationships with management, fellow EMTs, and volunteers
- Ability to take direction, follow instructions carefully, and delegate

Related Employment

Emergency Medical Technician, Mobile, AL   June 2009 to Present
- Perform patient assessment and provide advanced triage treatment
- Operate a variety of medical devices and equipment following approved treatment protocols
- Exchange information with nurses and doctors in the Emergency Room as well as between EMTs on incoming and outgoing shifts
- Check medical equipment, vehicles, and tools to ensure working order

Voluntary Firefighter, Rabun, AL   March 2008 to June 2009
- Maintained emergency vehicles such as fire trucks and ambulances
- Delivered public safety education
- Member of search-and-rescue and fire management operations teams

Technical Certifications and Degrees

Lurleen B. Wallace State Jr. College, Andalusia, AL
- EMT—Advanced, 2011
- EMT—Basic, 2009

Leadership Recognition

2011 recipient of the Outstanding Team Member Award for Leadership; Selected for prestigious EMT Accelerated Leadership Development Supervisor Training Program

Jacinda's Cover Letter and Resume

Jacinda Hernandez
1861 Hyacinth Street
Calabasas, CA 91302
818-555-6250
jhernandez@pax.com

February 6, 2012

Dr. Shirley Hamilton, Chair
College of Education
Paxen State University
Tuscon, AZ 85721

Dear Dr. Hamilton,

I am writing on the recommendation of Dr. Ribak, Professor of Curriculum and Instruction at Paxen State University. I recently discussed my upcoming relocation to the Tuscon area with Dr. Ribak and it was during our discussion that he mentioned an opening for an Assistant TESOL Professor in the College of Education. Dr. Ribak believes that I'd make an excellent candidate to fill this opening. I received my Ed.D. in Educational Leadership from the University of California, Los Angeles, in 2006, and am currently the ESL/ELL Program Coordinator for the Los Angeles Unified School District.

I have experience at every level of ESL/ELL programming, from classroom teacher to district-wide program coordinator. I began my career as an elementary school teacher and pursued my interest in ESL/ELL first as a resource teacher and then later as an ESL/ELL specialist. My work in the schools influenced my research interests in developing more efficient ESL/ELL programs.

My dissertation and research focus both on current best practices in ESL/ELL education and more specifically on effective implementation of these methodologies and successful integration with mainstream educational curriculum. The combination of my academic and professional experiences has uniquely prepared me for both research and teaching. My extensive knowledge of current practices in elementary education guides my research interests and helps me to prepare students who are studying to work in the field. I've spent the majority of my career connected in some way to the classroom. Whether working on reading skills with elementary school children or training colleagues in teaching methodologies, I've always enjoyed the challenges and rewards of classroom teaching. As ESL/ELL Program Coordinator, I've enjoyed the exchange of ideas with colleagues as well as leading and participating on organizational committees.

I look forward to sharing both my teaching and professional experience with the students and faculty at Paxen State University. To that end, enclosed please find copies of my CV, transcripts, and contact information for my professional references. I would be more than happy to provide any other documentation upon request.
I am available at the contact information listed above. Thank you for your consideration.

Respectfully,

Jacinda Hernandez

Jacinda Hernandez, Ed.D.
Enclosures: Curriculum Vitae, Transcripts, Professional References

Unlike our other candidates, all of whom are newer to the workforce, Jacinda counts more than 15 years of experience in her field. As a result, her cover letter and curriculum vitae, or CV, includes additional detail. Her CV alone runs three pages. To accommodate the extra content, Sandra selects a font, Garamond Pro, that enables her to squeeze more information into her letter and CV. Like Luis, Jacinda opens her letter with a personal reference and follows it with news of her impending move to the Tuscon area, near Paxen State University—strategies designed to encourage a hiring manager to read her CV.

Jacinda M. Hernandez, Ed.D.
1861 Hyacinth Street, Calabasas, CA 91302
(818) 555-6250
jhernandez@pax.com

Curriculum Vitae

CAREER OBJECTIVE: A skilled and qualified educational leader with years of teaching and leadership experience who seeks to use acquired knowledge and expertise to positively impact a college or university through effective organization, communication, and leadership.

PROFESSIONAL OVERVIEW—EDUCATIONAL LEADERSHIP

More than 20 years of experience in education

- ESL/ELL program coordination
- Direct support of classroom teachers
- Teacher staff development
- One-on-one work with students
- Classroom teaching experience
- ESL paraprofessional experience

EDUCATION AND CREDENTIALS

Ed.D., Educational Leadership, "An Analysis of ELL Program Integration: Examining Shared Traits of Successful Implementations," University of California, Los Angeles, 2006
M.A., Education, Educational Leadership and Administration, University of California, Los Angeles, 2002
B.S., Elementary Education, ELL Certification, University of the Pacific, 1996

PROFESSIONAL EXPERIENCE

Los Angeles Unified School District (LAUSD), Los Angeles, CA

ESL/ELL Program Coordinator (2006 to Present)
Design, implement, and coordinate ESL/ELL programming for LAUSD
Assess individual school programs and provided feedback. Organize ESL/ELL teacher training.
Achievement(s):
- Improved scores in reading and mathematics for all ESL/ELL learners in LAUSD over a 4-year period.

Itinerant ESL Teacher (2003 to 2006)
Provided ESL support in elementary classrooms; worked with individual students on reading and writing skills
Achievement(s):
- Reduced classroom discipline issues
- Increased integration of non-English speaking and English-speaking students
- Improved scores in reading and mathematics

San Luis Obispo School District, San Luis Obispo, CA

Itinerant ESL Teacher (2002 to 2003)
ESL/Reading Resource Teacher (1999 to 2002)
Provided ELL support in elementary classrooms; worked with individual students on reading and writing skills
Achievement(s):
- Improved scores in reading and mathematics
- Improved reading and writing skills

LESSON REVIEW

▶ Assessment

1. Explain ways in which your cover letter and resume should support one another.

2. Describe the formats you plan to use for your cover letter and resume. Also note and explain your choice of font and point size for both your cover letter and resume.

Pathways

Submitting Your Employment Essentials

Now that you know how to complete applications, resumes, and cover letters, you must learn the various ways in which to submit them.

- In a print version, you can set off text via various fonts, boldfaced or italic type, bulleted lists, and other formatting effects. You then may print the documents and mail or email them (as attachments) or deliver them by hand to hiring managers.

- In a plain-text or text-only version, you can copy and paste your resume or cover letter into online applicant-tracking systems.

HARD-COPY EMPLOYMENT ESSENTIALS

1 If your resume runs one page without enclosures, you should fold and mail it in a standard business envelope. If your resume exceeds one page or includes enclosures, you should mail the materials unfolded in a large manila envelope.

2 Double-check the name and address of the hiring manager on your documents. Then, label the envelope. A typed label appears more professional, but neat, legible handwriting also can be acceptable.

3 Regardless of the envelope that you use, ensure that it includes the correct amount of postage. If necessary, the post office can assist you with the proper amount of postage.

ELECTRONIC EMPLOYMENT ESSENTIALS

1 Ensure that you produce and save your documents in a word-processing application, such as Microsoft Word, that employers easily may access. If sending a Word document, use the most common file extension, such as *.doc.*

2 Employers may lack access to newer versions of Word that use *.docx* extensions. If you're in doubt about the employer's version of word-processing software, you always can play it safe by converting your formatted resume to a PDF.

3 If sending your resume as an attachment, you either may paste your cover letter into the viewing window of your email or submit it as a separate attachment. If an employer only accepts plain-text resumes and cover letters, you'll need to copy and paste your materials into an applicant-tracking system.

4 Finally, does the employer require a particular subject line or reference number to appear with the submission? If so, ensure that you type it exactly as it appears in the job advertisement. In some cases, it may appear in your email's subject line.

Hiring officials use applicant-tracking systems to view candidates and their profiles.

CHAPTER 3

Chapter Recap

Using the list below, place a checkmark next to the goals you achieved in Chapter 3.

▶ **In Lesson 1, you . . .**

- ☐ Learned the purpose of a cover letter
- ☐ Examined different types of cover letters
- ☐ Knew when to use each type of cover letter

▶ **In Lesson 2, you . . .**

- ☐ Learned the standard components of a cover letter
- ☐ Examined in detail the components of a cover letter
- ☐ Applied your knowledge by writing part of your cover letter

▶ **In Lesson 3, you . . .**

- ☐ Learned to properly format a cover letter
- ☐ Examined strategies for editing your cover letter
- ☐ Understood the importance of a professional, error-free cover letter

▶ **In Lesson 4, you . . .**

- ☐ Finalized your cover letter and resume

Chapter Review

Name: _____ **Date:** _____

▶ **Directions:** Match the terms in the left column to the correct definition in the right column.

_____ 1. networking letter

_____ 2. referral letter

_____ 3. letter of interest

_____ 4. internship letter

A. a type of cover letter in which the writer mentions in the opening paragraph the name of the person who referred them to the company or the hiring official

B. a type of cover letter in which the writer seeks a short-term, paid or unpaid position with a company in which he or she has interest

C. a type of cover letter in which the writer seeks to receive career advice and assistance

D. a type of cover letter in which the writer alerts a company and its hiring officials to his or her interest in working for them

▶ **Directions:** Determine whether the following statements are true or false. If the statement is true, write T. if the statement is false, write F. Then rewrite the false statement to make it true.

5. A candidate should write a letter of interest when seeking career advice and assistance.

_____

6. The main components of a cover letter are an opening salutation, an opening paragraph, middle paragraphs, a closing paragraph, and a closing salutation.

_____

▶ **Directions:** Write your answer to the question on the lines below.

7. Give an example of a strong opening salutation and a weak opening salutation in a cover letter. Explain how they differ.

_____

_____

8. Describe how a cover letter can help an applicant's candidacy for a position.

_____

_____

_____

▶ **Directions:** Read and edit the cover letter below. *(Hint: You should find and make 10 edits on this cover letter.)*

9.

Chad Carlton
1234 Bayou Boulevard
New Orleans, LA 70112

July 11, 2012

Mr. Dakota M. Patton
Drilling Specialists
55 Poydras Street
New Orleans, LA 70112

Dear Mr. Parton,

I'm writing you in response to Drilling Specialists' recent advertisement for a Drilling Engineer. Due to the current economic situation, Sunset Drilling has found it necessary to terminate my employment. While at Sunset Drilling, I worked closely with your company on many projects. In fact, I've long enjoyed a strong working relationship with your organization and I would like you to consider me for employment. My background would be an asset to you, especially in today's job market. Following please find a brief summary of my qualifications:

- Six years of field experience in cement slurry design and deep well placement
- Aided in development of Sunset Drilling's Slurry Placement Analysis program (cement job simulator)
- Three years of experience in supervising and operating cement test equipment (high-pressure consist-o-meter, fluid loss, autoclave, and so forth)
- Aided in development of a monitoring system that measures the U-tube effect during cement placement

In closing, I'd like to thank you in advance for your time and consideration. After you've had a chance to review my qualifications, I will call to hear your reactions.

Chad Carlton
Chad Carlton

Name: _____ Date: _____

▶ **Directions:** Use the reading and your own experience to complete the cover letter below.

10.

Your Contact Information:

_____

_____

_____

_____

_____

Date:

_____

Hiring Manager's Contact Information:

_____

_____

_____

_____

_____

_____

Opening Salutation:

_____

Opening Paragraph:

_____

_____

_____

Middle Paragraph:

_____

_____

_____

Middle Paragraph (if applicable):

_____

_____

_____

Closing Paragraph:

_____

_____

Closing Salutation:

_____

_____

Additional Resources

▶ **APPENDICES:**

    A: Job Application Checklist

    B: Active Verbs List

    C: Resume Checklist

    D. Cover Letter Checklist

    E: Tracking Tool

▶ **GLOSSARY**

▶ **ANSWER KEY**

▶ **INDEX**

Appendices

▶ **A: Job Application Checklist**

Job applications require candidates to supply a fair amount of documentation. Use the checklist below to ensure that you include information required by most job applications.

Personal Information:
- ☐ Name
- ☐ Address
- ☐ City, state, zip code
- ☐ Phone number
- ☐ Social Security number
- ☐ Driver's license
- ☐ Eligibility to work in the United States
- ☐ Felony convictions (if applicable)

Education:
- ☐ Schools/colleges attended and graduated
- ☐ Major
- ☐ Diploma/degree
- ☐ Graduation dates(s)

Position Information:
- ☐ Title of the job for which you're applying
- ☐ Hours per day/per week you're available to work
- ☐ Date on which you can start

Employment Information:
- ☐ Names, addresses, phone numbers of previous employers
- ☐ Supervisor's name and contact information
- ☐ Dates of employment
- ☐ Beginning and ending salary
- ☐ Reason for leaving

References:
- ☐ List of three references (names, job titles, and contact information)
- ☐ Resume (if you have one)

B: Active Verbs List

Following are a series of active verbs for use in your cover letter and resume.

Accomplish	Comply	Edit	Institute	Prepare	Secure
Accrue	Conceptualize	Educate	Instruct	Present	Select
Acquire	Conclude	Emphasize	Integrate	Prevent	Send
Achieve	Condense	Encourage	Interact	Print	Serve
Adapt	Conduct	Enforce	Interview	Prioritize	Shape
Address	Confer	Engineer	Introduce	Process	Share
Adjust	Configure	Enhance	Investigate	Produce	Showcase
Administer	Connect	Ensure	Itemize	Program	Simplify
Advertise	Conserve	Establish	Join	Promote	Solve
Advise	Consolidate	Estimate	Justify	Propose	Sort
Advocate	Construct	Evaluate	Launch	Prospect	Specialize
Aid	Consult	Examine	Learn	Prove	Specify
Alert	Contact	Execute	Lecture	Provide	Standardize
Align	Continue	Expand	Lead	Publicize	Start
Allocate	Contribute	Expedite	Lift	Publish	Streamline
Analyze	Control	Explain	Link	Purchase	Succeed
Appraise	Convert	Facilitate	Listen	Pursue	Suggest
Approve	Convey	Finance	Maintain	Qualify	Summarize
Assemble	Convince	Focus	Manage	Rate	Supervise
Assess	Coordinate	Forecast	Manipulate	Receive	Supply
Assign	Correspond	Formulate	Map	Recommend	Support
Assist	Counsel	Foster	Market	Reconcile	Surpass
Attain	Create	Fund	Measure	Record	Survey
Authorize	Critique	Gain	Mediate	Recruit	Sustain
Award	Cultivate	Generate	Mentor	Reduce	Target
Budget	Customize	Graduate	Merge	Refer	Teach
Build	Decide	Greet	Mobilize	Refocus	Test
Calculate	Declare	Guide	Modify	Regulate	Track
Campaign	Dedicate	Head	Monitor	Reorganize	Train
Certify	Define	Help	Motivate	Repair	Transform
Chair	Delegate	Hire	Negotiate	Replace	Translate
Change	Deliver	Host	Observe	Report	Transmit
Choose	Demonstrate	Identify	Obtain	Represent	Transport
Clarify	Describe	Illustrate	Open	Research	Tutor
Classify	Design	Implement	Operate	Resolve	Unify
Coach	Determine	Improve	Order	Respond	Update
Collaborate	Develop	Improvise	Organize	Restore	Upgrade
Collate	Devise	Increase	Originate	Restructure	Use
Collect	Diagnose	Influence	Outpace	Retrieve	Validate
Combine	Direct	Inform	Outperform	Review	Verify
Communicate	Dispatch	Initiate	Participate	Revise	View
Compare	Distribute	Innovate	Perform	Revitalize	Volunteer
Compile	Document	Inspire	Persuade	Run	Work
Complete	Draft	Install	Plan	Schedule	Write

Appendices

▶ **C: Resume Checklist**

Below are essential elements that your resume must include. Ensure that you check each box below before submitting your resume.

Components (Chapter 2, Lesson 1)

My Resume:

❐ features my current contact information, including street and email addresses and land line and cell phone numbers

❐ includes an objective statement customized for each opportunity

❐ summarizes my most impressive skills in a qualifications section

❐ lists my positions, duties, and responsibilities in reverse-chronological order

❐ contains relevant education, training, and certification

❐ spotlights relevant achievements and awards

Format / Appearance (Chapter 2, Lesson 2)

My Resume:

❐ uses a format, such as a skills resume, a reverse-chronological resume, a hybrid resume, or a curriculum vitae, that best reflects my background

❐ labels sections (e.g., *qualifications, work experience*) clearly throughout

❐ sequences sections properly to optimize my strengths and qualifications

❐ uses an appropriate point size and font

❐ reflects equal page margins on all sides

❐ incorporates design elements such as bullets, boldfaced type, and ruled lines to guide a hiring manager easily through my resume

❐ appears professional, clutter-free, and easy-to-read

Content (Chapter 2, Lesson 3)

My Resume:

❐ supports my career goal

❐ includes content relevant to a hiring manager's needs

❐ separates work responsibilities from accomplishments

❐ includes accomplishment statements that begin with a variety of active verbs

❐ quantifies my accomplishments by citing statistics, numbers, percentages, dollar amounts or other concrete measures of success

❐ flows logically

❐ spotlights keywords and sections

❐ features accurate statements throughout

❐ omits personal information such as age, race or ethnicity, and marital status

❐ reflects a polished, perfect document free of grammar or syntax errors

▶ D: Cover Letter Checklist

Below are essential elements that your cover letter must include. Ensure that you check each box below before submitting your cover letter.

Format (Chapter 3, Lesson 1)

My Cover Letter:

☐ uses a format, such as a job application cover letter, an interest / inquiry cover letter, a networking cover letter, a referral cover letter, or an internship cover letter, that best reflects my background

Components (Chapter 3, Lesson 2)

My Cover Letter:

☐ includes my current contact information, including street and email addresses and land line and cell phone numbers

☐ features the correct date

☐ uses an appropriate opening salutation, ideally with the name and title of the hiring official

☐ contains strong opening, middle, and closing paragraphs

☐ uses an appropriate closing salutation

Appearance (Chapter 3, Lesson 3)

My Cover Letter:

☐ uses an appropriate point size and font, ideally one that matches my resume

☐ reflects equal page margins on all sides

☐ incorporates design elements such as bullets, boldfaced type, and ruled lines to guide a hiring manager easily through my resume

☐ appears professional, clutter-free, and easy-to-read

Content (Chapter 3, Lesson 3)

My Cover Letter:

☐ supports my career goal and resume

☐ includes content relevant to a hiring manager's needs

☐ communicates my expertise via the use of strong active verbs and keywords

☐ quantifies my accomplishments by citing statistics, numbers, percentages, dollar amounts or other concrete measures of success

☐ flows logically

☐ ends with a call to action, such as a request for an interview

☐ includes my signature, either by hand or virtually by checking an electronic box

☐ lists any accompanying enclosures

☐ features accurate statements throughout

☐ omits personal information such as age, race or ethnicity, and marital status

Appendices

▶ **E: Tracking Tool–Career Web sites**

Use the table below to track your information on career Web sites.

CAREER SITES	Web Site #1	Web Site #2	Web Site #3
Web Site			
User Name			
Password (optional)			
Date Submitted			
Status of Submission			
Comments			

CAREER SITES	Web Site #4	Web Site #5	Web Site #6
Web Site			
User Name			
Password (optional)			
Date Submitted			
Status of Submission			
Comments			

▶ E: Tracking Tool–Networking Contacts

Use the table below to track your network of contacts.

NETWORKING CONTACTS

Acquaintance Information

Name/Title	Company Name	Contact Information	Date Contacted

Comments:

Lead Information	Lead 1	Lead 2	Lead 3
Lead Name/Title			
Company			
Contact Information			
Date Contacted			
Comments			

Appendices

▶ **E: Tracking Tool–Networking Contacts**

NETWORKING CONTACTS

Acquaintance Information

Name/Title	Company Name	Contact Information	Date Contacted

Comments:

Lead Information	Lead 1	Lead 2	Lead 3
Lead Name/Title			
Company			
Contact Information			
Date Contacted			
Comments			

NETWORKING CONTACTS

Acquaintance Information

Name/Title	Company Name	Contact Information	Date Contacted

Comments:

Lead Information	Lead 1	Lead 2	Lead 3
Lead Name/Title			
Company			
Contact Information			
Date Contacted			
Comments			

▶ E: Tracking Tool–Cover Letter/Resume

Use the table below to track your cover letter and resume submissions.

SUBMISSIONS	Job #1	Job #2	Job #3
Job Applied for			
Company Name			
Contact Name/Title			
Phone			
Fax			
Email Address			
Mailing Address			
Web Site			
Date Submitted			
How Submitted (Online, Mail, etc.)			
References Sent			
How Learned of Job			
Job Description/ Keywords			
Status of Application			
Comments			

SUBMISSIONS	Job #4	Job #5	Job #6
Job Applied for			
Company Name			
Contact Name/Title			
Phone			
Fax			
Email Address			
Mailing Address			
Web Site			
Date Submitted			
How Submitted (Online, Mail, etc.)			
References Sent			
How Learned of Job			
Job Description/ Keywords			
Status of Application			
Comments			

Appendices

▶ **E: Tracking Tool–Interviews**

Use the table below to track your interviews.

INTERVIEWS	Interview #1	Interview #2	Interview #3
Company			
Interview Date			
Interviewer Name/Title			
Email Address			
Phone Number			
Mailing Address			
Date of Follow-up Letter Submission			
Comments			

INTERVIEWS	Interview #4	Interview #5	Interview #6
Company			
Interview Date			
Interviewer Name/Title			
Email Address			
Phone Number			
Mailing Address			
Date of Follow-up Letter Submission			
Comments			

Glossary

A

applicant-tracking system: an electronic employer database that collects, stores, and sometimes even ranks applicant information

C

closing salutation: the end of a cover letter; the most commonly used closing salutations are "Sincerely," "Respectfully," "Regards," "Kind regards," and "Best regards"

components: parts

cover letter: an introductory letter to an employer that provides candidates with their first, best chance to communicate both their interest and expertise to hiring officials

curriculum vitae: a type of resume, commonly known as a CV, that emphasizes a candidate's academic achievements

E

education, training, and certification: information, such as major courses of study and degrees, that support a candidate's career decision

employment profile: an electronic file that contains much of the same information—contact numbers and work and education histories—as your resume

F

format: the way in which a document appears

H

hybrid resume: a resume that combines the format of a skills resume with that of a reverse-chronological resume

I

internship: a paid or unpaid position at a company in which you have interest

internship letter: a type of cover letter that explains to an employer a candidate's qualifications for an internship

J

job application: a print or electronic form that potential employees must complete to be considered by a company for employment

K

kiosks: small and open, free-standing structures that are booth-like, or desks with computers at which you can complete job applications

L

letter of interest: a type of cover letter, also known as a letter of inquiry or a prospecting letter, that alerts a company and its hiring manager to your interest in working for them

N

networking: the exchange of information or services among individuals, groups, or institutions

networking letter: a type of cover letter that requests career advice and assistance

O

objective statement: a summary of a candidate's skills and career goals

opening salutation: a greeting at the beginning of a cover letter or message that includes the name of the hiring official

P

PDF: portable document format

Q

qualifications section: a brief paragraph that summarizes a candidate's most impressive skills, abilities, and achievements as they relate to an opportunity

R

references: individuals who can speak to your ability to perform a particular job

referral letter: a type of cover letter that mentions in the opening paragraph the name of the person who referred you to a potential employer

resume: a career summary that describes an applicant's education, skills, work history, and expertise in relation to a specific job posting

reverse-chronological resume: a type of resume that emphasizes a candidate's employment experience and achievements by first listing the most recent (or current) position, then the next most recent, and so on

S

search engine: software applications such as Google, Bing, or Yahoo, used to locate documents and Web sites online

skills resume: a type of resume that emphasizes a candidate's strengths and skills rather than his or her experience

T

track: to follow

V

vocational training: training in a particular industry or position

W

white space: paragraph returns between lines

work experience: an employment summary that lists a candidate's positions, duties, responsibilities, and any honors or promotions they've earned

Answer Key

▶ **CHAPTER 1: Applications**

Lesson 1 Review

PAGE 19

1. A job application is a print or electronic form that potential employees must complete to be considered by a company for employment. Often, companies require candidates to complete applications so that the companies may compile a list of candidates and comply with state or federal hiring laws.

2. Applications require certain types of information from applicants. By following directions and supplying such information, applicants will be considered by an employer for a position. The ability of an applicant to follow directions in that context may suggest to an employer that person's ability to follow directions while on the job.

3. In a basic job application, a candidate must provide his or her full legal name, date of birth, driver's license and Social Security numbers, street and email addresses, and home and cell phone numbers. Other fields may require information from a candidate's most recent jobs, education history, and availability to work. In addition, nearly every application will ask whether a candidate is legally authorized to work in the United States and whether he or she has ever been convicted of a crime.

4. By signing and dating an application, a candidate attests to both its accuracy and its truthfulness.

5. A candidate seeking to make a strong first impression should dress appropriately for the potential work environment. For example, men should wear a dress shirt and slacks; women should wear the same or a business-appropriate dress. Further, a candidate should cover all tattoos, wear appropriate footwear (that which matches his or her pants and belt), and wash and style his or her hair. Women should apply an appropriate amount of make-up.

Lesson 2 Review

PAGE 25

1. Candidates may use the Internet to find job listings by typing the name of the company in which they're interested into a large search engine and adding the extension *.jobs* after it. In addition, large online job boards such as Monster.com and CareerBuilder.com feature thousands of job listings by category and city. Other online sites, such as snagajob.com and LinkUp.com, provide targeted lists of job openings by zip code. Candidates also can learn of job openings by routing directly to company Web sites and exploring listings under a tab such as "Employment" or "Careers." Finally, candidates may opt to apply online or at in-store kiosks.

2. By creating an online employment profile, candidates may house the same information—their contact numbers and work and education histories—along with their resume. Then, they can set up a profile that allows them to receive email alerts when the company adds new jobs to its site. That way, they can view and apply for jobs quickly.

3. Candidates should review and print electronic applications prior to their submission to ensure accuracy and avoid the presence of any errors that might otherwise remove them from consideration.

4. Through multiple-choice and open-ended questions, pre-employment tests help an employer determine whether a particular candidate will be a good fit for their company or for a specific job.

Chapter 1 Review

PAGES 29–32

1. C
2. A
3. B
4. D
5. B
6. D
7. T
8. F; Because most kiosks are located at stores or companies, their applications most likely will be specific to that store or company. The application also may be specific to a certain job at that company.

9. By tracking the positions for which they've applied, candidates can check the status of their application at any time.

10. Job applications include basic requirements, such as a candidate's full legal name, date of birth, driver's license and Social Security numbers, street and email addresses, and home and cell phone numbers. Other fields may require information from a candidate's most recent jobs, education history, and availability to work. In addition, nearly every application will ask whether a candidate is legally authorized to work in the United States and whether he or she ever has been convicted of a crime. Other, more detailed applications may request more job-specific information, such as a candidate's knowledge of certain software or any certifications he or she may hold. Still others may require candidates to complete a pre-employment test as part of their overall application.

11. Candidates may use the Internet in a variety of ways to seek and apply for jobs. For starters, candidates may locate job listings by typing the name of the company in which they're interested into a large search engine and adding the extension *.jobs* after it. They also may access large online job boards such as Monster.com and CareerBuilder.com, which combine to feature thousands of job listings by category and city. Similarly, other online sites, such as snagajob.com and LinkUp.com, provide targeted openings by zip code. Candidates also may learn of job openings by routing directly to company Web sites and exploring listings under a tab such as "Employment" or "Careers." Finally, candidates may apply for jobs in person, through traditional mail, via an applicant-tracking system, or at in-store kiosks.

12. Candidates first should read the application to learn the type and amount of information the company wants. Next, candidates should ensure that they complete all fields, especially those that include a star or asterisk (*) next to them. In particular, candidates should customize their information to the opening for which they're applying. In some cases, an applicant-tracking system may allow them to upload a resume or cover letter. As appropriate, candidates should list personal and professional references who can speak to their ability to perform a particular job. After candidates have completed the application, they should proofread it for errors. Employers often require that candidates sign an application to verify its accuracy. If they're applying through an applicant-tracking system, they may only need to click a button on the site prior to submission.

13. Responses will vary, but should reflect a comprehensive understanding of the chapter.

▶ **CHAPTER 2: Resumes**

Lesson 1 Review

PAGE 55
1. Standard resume components include the candidate's contact information, objective statement, qualifications section, work experience, education/training/certification, and achievements and awards.

2. Responses will vary, but should demonstrate an objective statement that, in one to three sentences, summarizes the candidate's skills and career goals for an employer.

3. Candidates should customize their resumes to the position for which they're applying by including keywords that match those in the job posting. Applicant-tracking systems and hiring managers will scan for keywords, which enable hiring officials to quickly identify an applicant's qualifications. If your resume includes certain keywords, you may advance to a phone or an in-person interview. If it lacks them, however, you may be eliminated from consideration.

4. A qualifications section summarizes in a brief paragraph a candidate's most impressive skills, abilities, and achievements as they relate to an opportunity. Qualifications statements—also known as summaries of qualifications—reflect employer needs rather than the individual goals present in objective statements.

Answer Key

5. Achievements in a resume help quantify a candidate's accomplishments to hiring officials, while awards provide third-party validation to their efforts.
6. Qualifications sections tend to include higher-level information (*Increased year-over-year sales*), while achievements sections tend to be more detailed (*Increased sales by 33 percent through the addition of independent sales representatives*).

Lesson 2 Review

PAGE 65
1. A candidate with both experience and skills should use a hybrid resume format.
2. The best format for a candidate with extensive academic achievements would be a curriculum vitae, or CV.
3. Responses will vary, but should be supported by information from the text.

Lesson 3 Review

PAGE 69
1. An ASCII plain-text resume contains the same information as a formatted resume but lacks much of the formatting common to word-processing documents. Today, many companies use applicant-tracking systems to record and rank their candidates. Many of these systems accept both formatted and ASCII plain-text resumes. Some, however, only accept ASCII resumes, which can be "read" by applicant-tracking systems.
2. Most plain-text resumes generally share the following features: a simple, plain-text font, such as Courier 12 point; limited formatting through the use of capital letters, asterisks (in place of bullets), and keyboard symbols; text justified to the left; white space to break up the text; and line lengths of 80 characters (the total letters, numbers, and spaces per line) or less.
3. Sandra next should choose the location in which to save her file, after which she should first open her word-processing program and then reopen the plain-text or *.txt* resume.
4. Responses will vary, but should reflect ideas and steps from the lesson.

Chapter 2 Review

PAGES 73–76
1. A
2. C
3. D
4. B
5. B
6. D
7. C
8. F; Although candidates may choose a resume format based on their level of experience, they'll include the same components regardless of format.
9. T
10. Candidates writing the work experience section of their resume likely will use a chronological format, in which candidates list their most recent (or current) position first, followed by their next most recent position, and so on. For each position, they'll list beginning and ending employment dates (by year and by month) next to or beneath each job title, followed by a summary of their duties and responsibilities. They'll begin each work experience entry with active verbs—present-tense verbs for current activities and past-tense for previous ones.
11. Responses will vary, but should reflect a comprehensive understanding of the chapter.

▶ CHAPTER 3: Cover Letters

Lesson 1 Review

PAGE 83
1. A cover letter enables a candidate to provide context about the positions, achievements, and career goals listed on his or her resume. In many ways, a well-written cover letter should draw a hiring official's attention to a candidate's resume.
2. An inquiry letter alerts a company and its hiring manager to your interest in working for them. A networking letter requests career advice and assistance from your friends, family members, and former co-workers.
3. By mentioning the name of the referral in the opening paragraph, a candidate immediately grabs the attention of the hiring official.

4. Responses will vary, but should reflect a comprehensive understanding of the lesson.

Lesson 2 Review

PAGE 95
1. Standard components of a cover letter include an opening salutation; an opening paragraph; middle paragraphs; a closing paragraph; and a closing salutation.
2. A well-written opening and closing salutation can set an effective tone—formal, familiar, or somewhere in between—for the rest of your letter.
3. Responses may vary, but could reflect that a candidate may include only one middle paragraph if he or she lacks significant work experience.
4. A candidate who states that he or she plans to contact the hiring official in a specified amount of time demonstrates further interest in the position and also establishes next steps in the hiring process.
5. Responses will vary, but should reflect a comprehensive understanding of the lesson.

Lesson 3 Review

PAGE 109
1. Candidates want to keep the focus of their cover letter on the content, and therefore should avoid using fancy fonts or intricate designs that could distract a hiring manager. In addition, hiring officials usually discard applications that include photographs, since they may invite racial or gender discrimination lawsuits from applicants.
2. A formatted cover letter uses an easy-to-read font, such as Arial or Verdana, and effects such as boldfaced and italicized type to emphasize certain points. It also may include tabs to justify information. In contrast, a plain-text cover letter features minimal formatting. It usually only includes capital letters, asterisks, keyboard symbols, and white space. However, plain-text cover letters may be "read" by applicant-tracking systems, whereas formatted resumes usually cannot.
3. You should use a spell-check function to catch spelling errors in your cover letter, after which you should ensure the opening salutation includes the correct

name, title, and street address of the hiring official to whom you're sending the cover letter. You may check the accuracy of the contact's name, title, and address by using a professional networking site such as LinkedIn. From there, you should check details in your letter, such as the title of the position for which you're applying. Finally, you should run another spell check, after which you should print and review it to eliminate any remaining errors in spelling, grammar, punctuation, or accuracy.
4. A professional, error-free cover letter presents an individual's candidacy in the best possible light and may urge a hiring official to take action by reading the companion resume and/or contacting the candidate for an interview.

Lesson 4 Review

PAGE 119
1. A resume and cover letter should support one another by extending and reiterating a candidate's qualifications, achievements, and/or career goals.
2. Responses will vary, but should reflect a comprehensive understanding of the material.

Chapter 3 Review

PAGES 123–126
1. C
2. A
3. D
4. B
5. F; A candidate should write a networking cover letter when seeking career advice and assistance.
6. T
7. A strong opening salutation reflects research and customization through the inclusion of a hiring official's correctly spelled name and accurate title, usually prefaced by the word "Dear." A weak opening salutation shows little research and customization, usually reflected in a generic opening such as "Dear Sir or Madam."

▶ **CHAPTER 3 (continued)**

8. Many candidates neglect to include a cover letter with their applications or resumes. Those that do, have an opportunity to provide context to their jobs, achievements, and career goals in a cover letter. Although a well-written cover letter won't guarantee a candidate a job, a poorly written one can eliminate them from consideration. In many ways, a well-written cover letter should draw a hiring official's attention to a candidate's resume.

9. Please see the below list and companion edited cover letter *(right)* for recommended responses.

   1. Chad included a primary phone number and email address at which he can be reached.
   2. Chad correctly spelled the last name of the hiring official, Mr. Parton.
   3. Chad included Mr. Parton's title, Senior Recruitment Consultant.
   4. Chad deleted information surrounding his departure from Sunset Drilling, which could distract Mr. Parton. Instead, he rewrote that section to reflect his 10-year tenure at Sunset—which helps to demonstrate his longevity—and his desire to explore new opportunities.
   5. Chad removed the redundancy "I would like you to consider me for employment," since the letter alone shows proof of that. In its place, he included supporting information about how he has "admired Drilling Specialists from afar," which suggests his genuine interest in their organization.
   6. Chad referenced his enclosed resume while removing the unnecessary comments about "today's job market."
   7. Chad indented supporting statements for his duties and responsibilities, which helps a hiring official like Mr. Parton navigate his letter.
   8. Chad provided a defined date and time on which he will follow up by phone with Mr. Parton, which shows Chad's organization, interest, and desire.
   9. Chad included a popular closing salutation, *Kind Regards*.
   10. Chad referenced the enclosure of his resume with the cover letter.

10. Responses will vary, but should reflect a comprehensive understanding of the chapter.

Answer Key for Editing a Cover Letter

Chad Carlton
1234 Bayou Boulevard
New Orleans, LA 70112
① (504) 555-5305
ccarlton@yahoo.com

July 11, 2012

Mr. Dakota M. Parton ②
③ Senior Recruitment Consultant
Drilling Specialists
55 Poydras Street
New Orleans, LA 70112

Dear Mr. Parton,

I'm writing you in response to Drilling Specialists' recent advertisement for a Drilling Engineer. ④ ~~Due to the current economic situation, Sunset Drilling has found it necessary to terminate my employment.~~ I recently left Sunset Drilling after nearly 10 years and am exploring other opportunities in the drilling industry. While at Sunset Drilling, I worked closely with your company on many projects. In fact, I've long enjoyed a strong working relationship with your organization and ⑤ ~~I would like you to consider me for employment~~ have admired Drilling Specialists from afar. My background and experience, as reflected in the ⑥ enclosed resume, would be an asset to you~~, especially in today's job market~~. Following please find a brief summary of my qualifications:

- Six years of field experience in cement slurry design and deep well placement
  › ⑦ Aided in development of Sunset Drilling's Slurry Placement Analysis program (cement job simulator)
- Three years of experience in supervising and operating cement test equipment (high-pressure consist-o-meter, fluid loss, autoclave, and so forth)
  › Aided in development of a monitoring system that measures the U-tube effect during cement placement

In closing, I'd like to thank you in advance for your time and consideration. ⑧ I'll plan to follow up with you by phone next Thursday, July 19, at 10 a.m. ET to answer any questions you may have.

⑨ Kind Regards,

Chad Carlton

Chad Carlton
⑩ Enclosure: Resume

Note: Page numbers in **bold** indicate definitions.

Index

Monster.com, 20, 29, 66

Index